DEAR READERS
AND RIDERS

ALSO BY
LETTIE TEAGUE

Wine in Words
Educating Peter
Fear of Wine

DEAR READERS AND RIDERS

The Beloved Books, Faithful Fans, and Hidden Private Life of Marguerite Henry

—— A BIOGRAPHY BY ——
LETTIE TEAGUE

T
TRAFALGAR SQUARE
North Pomfret, Vermont

First published in 2024 by
Trafalgar Square Books
North Pomfret, Vermont 05053

Disclaimer of Liability
The author and publisher shall have neither liability nor responsibility to any person
or entity with respect to any loss or damage caused or alleged to be caused directly or indirectly by
the information contained in this book. While the book is as accurate
as the author can make it, there may be errors, omissions, and inaccuracies.

The authors and publisher have made every effort to obtain a release from photographers whose
images appear in this book. In some cases, however, the photographers were not known or could
not be contacted. Should additional photographers be identified,
they will be credited in future editions of this book.

Trafalgar Square Books encourages the use of approved safety helmets in all equestrian
sports and activities.

Trafalgar Square Books certifies that the content in this book was generated by a human expert
on the subject, and the content was edited, fact-checked, and proofread by human publishing
specialists with a lifetime of equestrian knowledge. TSB does not publish books generated by
artificial intelligence (AI).

Library of Congress Cataloging-in-Publication Data
Names: Teague, Lettie, author.
Title: Dear readers and riders : the beloved books, faithful fans, and
  hidden private life of Marguerite Henry / a biography by Lettie Teague.
Description: North Pomfret, Vermont : Trafalgar Square Books, 2024. |
  Includes bibliographical references and index.
Identifiers: LCCN 2024002404 (print) | LCCN 2024002405 (ebook) | ISBN
  9781646011940 (paperback) | ISBN 9781646011957 (epub)
Subjects: LCSH: Henry, Marguerite, 1902-1997. | Authors, American--20th
  century--Biography. | Women authors, American--20th century--Biography.
Classification: LCC PS3515.E5784 Z893 2024 (print) | LCC PS3515.E5784
  (ebook) | DDC 813/.54 [B]--dc23/eng/20240206
LC record available at https://lccn.loc.gov/2024002404
LC ebook record available at https://lccn.loc.gov/2024002405

All photographs courtesy of the private collection of Marguerite Henry, except
where noted.

Letters on chapter frontispieces courtesy of the Marguerite Henry Collection,
The Kerlan, University of Minnesota Archives.

Illustrations from the original editions of the works of Marguerite Henry reprinted with permission
from Simon & Schuster Children's Publishing.

The main cover photo, courtesy of the private collection of Marguerite Henry, originally appeared
in the book *Dear Readers and Riders* by Marguerite Henry (Rand McNally, 1969).

Book design by *Katarzyna Misiukanis–Celińska (https://misiukanis-artstudio.com)*
Cover design by *RM Didier* | Index by *Andrea Jones (JonesLiteraryServices.com)*
Typefaces: *Adobe Text Pro* and *Perpetua Titling MT*

Printed in the United States of America

10 9 8 7 6 5 4 3 2 1

FOR ALL THE READERS WHO ARE RIDERS
AND ALL THE RIDERS WHO ARE READERS
AND ANYONE WHOSE CHILDHOOD
TREASURES WERE BOOKS

CONTENTS

WESLEY DENNIS

A REMARKABLE WOMAN
WHO WROTE
REMARKABLE BOOKS

"Nothing ever dies as long as there is the memory
to enfold it and a heart to love it."

—

GRANDMA BEEBE, *MISTY OF CHINCOTEAGUE*
(FIRST PUBLISHED 1947)

IN my favorite photograph of famed children's book author Marguerite Henry, the one that appears on the cover of this book, she's seated at her desk before a wide picture window, rather formally attired in a long-sleeved blouse, her hair swept up in an impressive beehive. The window behind her reveals bare trees and a flat, barren lawn: the Midwest in winter. There is a rotary phone on the desk and a globe just beyond it. The desk is piled high with papers and letters, and Marguerite has a bemused half-smile as she reads—or affects to read—a postcard.

This photograph first appeared in one of Marguerite's printed newsletters, which often opened with the salutation, *"Dear Readers and Riders."* The newsletters—of which there were only nine—were produced in the 1960s by her then-publisher Rand McNally to help respond to the flood of correspondence that Marguerite's books inspired and to promote her new works that were soon to be published (they helped accomplish the latter but did nothing to slow the former). These newsletters were later incorporated into a book by the same title (published in 1969—long before this one!) that shared her responses to readers' questions about her books, and horses in general.

The photograph of Marguerite at her desk was taken at her home in Wayne, Illinois, and the lawn in the photograph is the wide expanse of grass that Marguerite dubbed "Mole Meadow." This was the fittingly fanciful address for a children's book author and the address to which readers sent thousands upon thousands of letters and postcards.

No house number nor street name was necessary: Marguerite's name, Mole Meadow, and the town of Wayne was enough. Her fame was that great and the town was that small. Marguerite's readers were mostly, but not entirely, young girls between the ages of eight and fifteen. Along with the letters and postcards, they sent photographs of themselves or their pets—usually dogs, occasionally cats, but almost always a horse or two. Sometimes readers sent pictures of themselves surrounded by veritable herds of plastic model equines, invariably based on the horses that starred in Marguerite's books. These toys were churned out by the millions by Breyer Animal Creations, a company specializing in models of horses, famous and otherwise, and were collected as avidly by horse lovers as the books that helped bring the horses to life.

Marguerite's correspondents importuned her to *"Please write back,"* or more urgently, *"Respond as soon as you can,"* or in the case of a more realistic or perhaps more business-like fan: *"Please respond within thirty days."* Her readers signed their correspondence *"With love,"* or *"Your friend,"* or *"Your devoted friend,"* or even *"Your number one fan"* in an effort to stand out from the crowd. Their desire for connection was blunt, forthright, and clearly expectant. *Of course* their favorite author would write back. And she did.

Marguerite answered in a tone that was familiar and warm, never condescending. Her letters were written as if she and her correspondent were the same age, and as such, she understood their concerns, their desires, and their frequent disappointments (horses figured largely in all three). But it wasn't just that Marguerite understood what her fans wrote; she truly felt their words of love, longing, and sometimes despair as if they were her own—perhaps because they often were.

Marguerite never thought of herself as the "adult" and the reader as the "child"; they were one and the same, together in their feelings, and almost invariably, their love of horses. *"I understand how you feel,"* she wrote, relaying some similar incident or feeling of her own. Sometimes the letters were about a child's trouble at home or difficulty at school, or they solicited a practical piece of advice about saddle fit or stirrup position or how to deal with a stubborn horse. Often as not, her readers described a terrible, aching longing for a horse of their own—an ache Marguerite knew herself.

Although they were not her only subjects, horses and ponies loomed large in Marguerite's substantial oeuvre of books, and the lawn that appears in the window just beyond Marguerite in that iconic photograph wasn't actually a meadow but an improvised stage for all sorts of celebrations, primarily centered around one very high-profile pony named Misty who lived with Marguerite for just over a decade but brought her a lifetime of fame.

Misty was the namesake and star of *Misty of Chincoteague*, Marguerite's most famous and bestselling book, first published in 1947 and still very much in print and very much beloved to this day. A blend of real life and fiction, *Misty* told the story of a real boy and girl—and a real pony born on an island of wild ponies off the coast of Virginia. The protagonists were real but the story of what happened to them all was the product of Marguerite's marvelous imagination and pellucid prose. The book not only became a bestseller translated in multiple languages but also a 1961 movie and one of those popular plastic model horses produced by Breyer Animal Creations. It was also the source of a veritable tourism tsunami of passionate pony lovers who now descend upon the small island of Chincoteague every July on "Pony Penning Day"—and all the months before and after as well.

Books like *Misty of Chincoteague*—a clever combination of real-life stories of horses and children coupled to intensive historical and scholarly research—had few parallels in the world of children's books back in those days, and still have few today. Marguerite's storytelling ability and diligent research were as singular as her prose and the reason why her work was both beloved and respected, and why her books are remembered by so many, even now. It is my hope that this biography might help reveal just how Marguerite Henry the writer was every bit as remarkable as the books that she wrote.

And now an admission: although Marguerite wrote fifty-nine books, not every book she wrote was equal in merit. Sometimes she turned out more than one book a year, and some books were comprehensive while others were comparatively slight. In these pages I've chosen to highlight the books that represent, to me, not only some of the best of Marguerite Henry's work, but also those that help best tell the story of Marguerite Henry herself.

Lettie Teague

letters

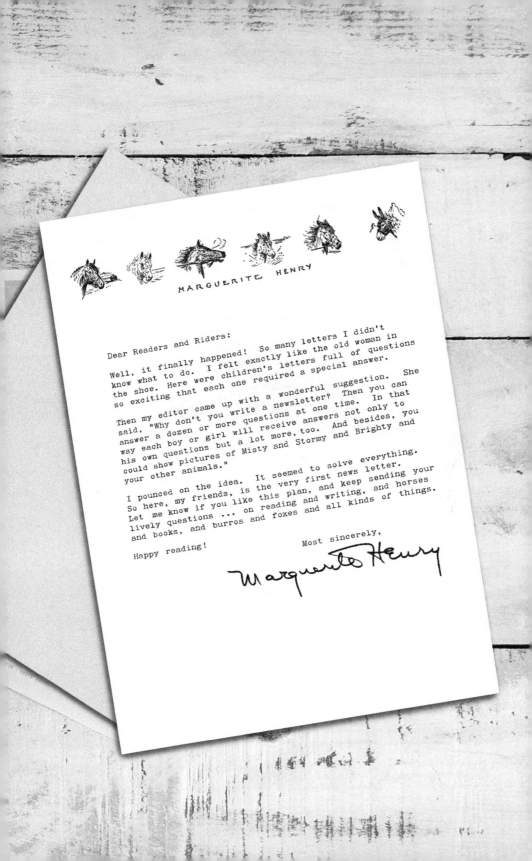

MARGUERITE HENRY

Dear Readers and Riders:

Well, it finally happened! So many letters I didn't know what to do. I felt exactly like the old woman in the shoe. Here were children's letters full of questions so exciting that each one required a special answer.

Then my editor came up with a wonderful suggestion. She said, "Why don't you write a newsletter? Then you can answer a dozen or more questions at one time. In that way each boy or girl will receive answers not only to his own questions but a lot more, too. And besides, you could show pictures of Misty and Stormy and Brighty and your other animals."

I pounced on the idea. It seemed to solve everything. So here, my friends, is the very first news letter. Let me know if you like this plan, and keep sending your lively questions ... on reading and writing, and horses and books, and burros and foxes and all kinds of things.

Happy reading!

Most sincerely,

Marguerite Henry

1

THE EARLY YEARS: AT HOME IN MILWAUKEE AND OUT IN THE WORLD

1

*"By the early 20ᵗʰ century Milwaukee
had developed a national reputation based
on three related hallmarks:
Germanism, Socialism and beer."*

—

THE MILWAUKEE COUNTY HISTORICAL SOCIETY

W hen celebrity prohibitionist Carrie Nation (famous for rather cinematically smashing up barrooms with her hatchet) visited Wisconsin in 1902, she declared, "If there is any place that is hell on earth, it is Milwaukee." Marguerite Henry née Breithaupt, born in Milwaukee that same year, would likely have disagreed.

The Milwaukee of Marguerite's childhood was a dynamic, progressive city almost as famous for its socialist politics as its bars and its beer. The latter two incited Ms. Nation's fury while the city's first socialist mayor, elected a few years later, made Milwaukee into one of the great cosmopolitan cities of the Midwest in the early twentieth century.

One of Milwaukee's most important assets was its large well-educated German population. In the years just before World War I, the city was dubbed the "German Athens," according to Milwaukee historian and author John Gurda, and Germans held great stature there. "It was very easy to be German in Milwaukee," Mr. Gurda observed.

Marguerite's paternal grandparents were both born in Germany; her father Louis was a Milwaukee native. When Marguerite was born, her parents lived on the less fashionable west side of the city where the houses were tidy if tightly spaced, but as the family's fortunes improved, and their household multiplied in number, the Breithaupts moved east to a more spacious house with a decidedly larger lawn.

Marguerite's father ran his family's printing business, and the adult Marguerite recalled her childhood visits to L. Breithaupt Printing Company in downtown Milwaukee with a mixture of joy and awe. Her father's business, with its presses and reams of paper of all colors, was a place "more exciting than Pandora's box," recalled Marguerite— and her father was, to her, rather exciting too. *Everyone noticed when Papa wrote. And everyone listened when he yodeled or sang folk songs or recited whole passages from Shakespeare,"* Marguerite wrote in a hand-typed essay she had titled "Things I Remember."

Marguerite was a grateful recipient of her father's largesse—when she visited his office, there was a seemingly endless supply of pencils and paper available for her use, and he showered his youngest daughter regularly with these small precious gifts. Louis Breithaupt's place of business was a dream world for an aspiring writer—in fact, it was just a dream for Marguerite when she was housebound with rheumatic fever from ages six to twelve.

While Marguerite's descriptions of her father are loving and deeply felt, the memories of her mother Anna are less precise—gently admiring but less intense. Marguerite's recollections of her mother have mostly to do with her appearance, especially her elegance in movement and stature. Her mother *"carried her head like an Arabian,"* Marguerite wrote—an unorthodox description of one's parent, perhaps, but one befitting an author of horse books.

Louis liked to have his children visit his printing company regularly, particularly on Saturdays. Marguerite's sister Gertrude recalled the stacks of paper and multi-colored tiers of colored tablets that were everywhere as a family joke of sorts. *"Papa never said, 'A penny for your thoughts'; always it was, 'A tablet for your thoughts'!"* she recounted. Gertrude was the youngest of Marguerite's three older sisters and the sister to whom Marguerite was especially close. Indeed, Gertrude was her "mother-confessor," her "unabridged dictionary," and later, her unofficial editor and best reader of her books. *"Editors could be wrong but not Gertrude,"* Marguerite noted.

A Housebound Life

The sisters' bond was made tighter by the fact of Marguerite's terrible illness. Rheumatic fever—an inflammation of the heart that often followed a respiratory ailment—was one of the leading causes of death in young people around the turn of the twentieth century. Two of Marguerite's older brothers died young; the first, Louis, in 1884, before Marguerite was born, and Lorenz the year after her birth—he was only seven years old; the cause of death was "measles and pneumonia."

Under such circumstances it's understandable that Marguerite's mother wanted first and foremost to keep her youngest daughter safe. Since the only "cure" for Marguerite's illness in those days was complete rest, her diagnosis led to six years of housebound life. This not only brought Gertrude and Marguerite closer but helped turn

Marguerite into a reader and writer—as did the red writing table that her father gave her when she was nine or ten years old.

Stocked with her favorite gift of paper and pencils, the desk, which her father set up in a corner of the kitchen, was Marguerite's own personal kingdom. She recalled the moment she first saw the desk in an edition of her newsletter: *"What caught my eye first was my own cream pitcher, holding a bright bouquet of pencils.... Brand new, they were, with their erasers firm and unchewed, and all so freshly sharpened that to this day the memory of their cedarwood fragrance tickles my nose."* They would remain some of the very same tools that Marguerite would wield for the rest of her life. She wrote all her books—and their many, many revisions, along with her voluminous notes—with a pencil on paper before they were typed, either by herself, or more often, an assistant. It was a practice she maintained for almost eighty years.

Seated at her tiny kitchen desk under the watchful eye of her mother, Marguerite wrote stories that she later noted were "for adults" rather than children, although she offered no examples of her childhood work, alas. The close proximity of her mother while she wrote in those early years may have influenced Marguerite's wish for company wherever she wrote later on—whether it was her siblings or later her husband Sid or one of her many dogs. Marguerite also wrote under the watchful eye of countless librarians who were one of the greatest constants of Marguerite's work and life. Librarians were dependable, quiet company, as well as reliable researchers to whom Marguerite could turn with one of her endless requests for more information. Marguerite owed a great deal of her work to their efforts, and she repaid their numerous favors by extolling the virtues of libraries and librarians in her interviews and making regular appearances at libraries and related conventions all over the country. Some of the librarians she worked with the most became such good friends that they even offered to help Marguerite with her research *after* they retired from their library posts. The devotion was clearly mutual.

Many years after she had become a successful children's book author, Marguerite described her early childhood years with great nostalgia, imparting a warm glow to what surely must have been some lonely years, deprived of companions close to her own age. All her siblings, save for Gertrude, were much older than Marguerite. She referred to them as *"grownups"* and said they were less like having sisters and a brother than *"a whole flock of mothers and fathers."*

First Publication

While Marguerite wrote stories for her own amusement and that of her family in the beginning, she soon decided she should try to get her work published. Marguerite had found a solicitation for short stories based on the four seasons in one of her mother's magazines and decided to submit a story of her own. She wrote about visiting a friend in the country when she was well enough to venture out.

The season she chose to focus on was the fall, and Marguerite described the experience of jumping into a pile of leaves during a game of hide and seek. It was the perfect hiding place, Marguerite thought, until her friend's dog gave her location away. That story—"Hide and Seek Through the Autumn Leaves"—was published in *The Woman's Home Companion* (or *The Delineator*—sources vary) and Marguerite was paid the quite-handsome sum of twelve dollars or nearly four hundred dollars in today's money. (Oddly enough, in her Rand McNally author biography, the amount is noted as "the full sum of one dollar" or eleven dollars less than the number Marguerite herself cited as payment.)

Marguerite didn't keep a copy of her very first work, and it's proven impossible to track down, although her fans have tried to find it over the years. (The story was a Reddit forum topic for a while as fans searched for it in vain.) Marguerite wrote that she often wished that she had kept a copy of the story, and those first few dollars, too, since it was the first money she earned in her writing career.

Having her very first effort published so quickly and easily gave Marguerite an unreasonable idea as to how easy writing for money would be, and so she conceived a bold childhood plan to become a writer and "buy a whole ranchful of horses" with the earnings from her books. Marguerite did, of course, get a horse and more than one ranch house in her life, but it took some time—many more years and many more books than she might have expected to achieve such success.

Dreams of Horses...and Other Things

The "ranchful of horses" that Marguerite hoped to own one day was a wish she rarely dared express as a child. No one in her family had a horse, save for her older brother Fred, whose horse Bonnie was bad-tempered and inclined to bite. Even so, Marguerite envied her brother for having Bonnie. Marguerite told *The Los Angeles Times* in 1992, *"I'm afraid I hated my brother because he used to smell so good. He smelled like horses."* She was so jealous in those early years that Marguerite made it a point to avoid all horses, although her passion did spill out in unexpected ways. In a speech at a 1979 reading conference in Indiana, Marguerite recalled how she would dash into telegraph offices and write "telegrams to the world" when she was a child. Her telegrams often as not included a sketch of a horse's head and these words: *"I look into your great brown eyes/and wonder where the difference lies/Between your soul and mine."*

There were quite a few horses around on the streets of Milwaukee in Marguerite's early years. Horses were used not only for transportation but vital city work, especially sanitation. There were horses used for picking up garbage in Milwaukee as late as 1957 when the last so-called "garbage horse" Dolly finally retired. (Sadly, Dolly's existence seems to have gone unremarked-upon by Marguerite, though the hard life of a city garbage horse seems like a very Marguerite sort of book.)

When her readers asked Marguerite to describe her childhood, and especially the horses of her youth, she told them about Bonnie (complete with the fact of Bonnie's very bad temperament). *"But what about your own horse?"* her readers asked. This seemed to be a very important point for them. Marguerite explained (repeatedly) to this evergreen question that she'd had to wait until she was a grownup to get a horse, and if her readers had to wait too, they would probably appreciate their horses that much more, just as she did. Interestingly, Marguerite never mentioned the fact she'd had to spend much of her early life sequestered at home so that riding, let alone horse ownership, was out of the question. Perhaps she wanted to recast the story of her childhood in the same way she had recast parts of the stories of the boys and girls and horses of her books. Her renditions may not have been completely factual, but they were entirely true to how she felt.

Aside from horses, the other topic that young Marguerite wrote about quite often was clothes—specifically, the hand-me-down attire from her sisters. Marguerite recalled a particularly sad piece of clothing—a black astrakhan coat—that she despised. The long fleecy lambskin had become quite bedraggled by the time it reached Marguerite, its third and last owner, and it didn't help that Marguerite was exceedingly thin. The effect was scarecrow-like and decidedly unflattering—a tattered garment draped on her thin frame, as she recalled.

Perhaps such sad childhood outfits helped to inform Marguerite's impeccable grownup attire. Photographs of the adult Marguerite invariably show her quite fashionably dressed in form-fitting jodhpurs or a snappy two-piece suit and sometimes even a fur coat, with her hair always, always impeccably coiffed under a hat. Marguerite was mad for hats—some quite plain, some rather sophisticated, others downright wild.

While Marguerite could be self-conscious about her appearance, she was just as likely to forget herself—and the world around her—while composing a story in her head. Her sister Gertrude described Marguerite as impossibly dreamy, so dreamy that she could literally lose track of her feet. Gertrude, whom Marguerite called "mom sister," had to watch out for her younger sister while she was doing something as simple as crossing the street.

There was one near-tragic instance of this dreaminess that Marguerite later described as a great opportunity. She had been roller-skating to the local library about a mile from her house, pretending that she was Hans Brinker, the hero of the book *Hans Brinker, or The Silver Skates* that she'd recently checked out of the library. In Marguerite's mind she wasn't a girl on a street in a midwestern city but Hans Brinker, skating on the ice in the Netherlands. (Interestingly, *Hans*, first published in 1865, was written by an American who hadn't visited the Netherlands until years after the book debuted.)

In this dreamlike state, young Marguerite skated off the street and into a passing motorcyclist. Fortunately, she received only minor injuries, but the book fared much worse. When Marguerite shamefacedly presented the damaged book to the librarian in charge, a young woman named Delia G. Ovitz, she was filled with trepidation, having read the notice in the book's inner flap that warned borrowers who damaged a book might be disbarred from the library. Marguerite, distraught, took the threat to heart. (Library books were much more valuable years ago when few could afford to buy their own books.)

But instead of disbarring Marguerite, Ms. Ovitz brought her into the room where the library books were repaired to show Marguerite how the book that she had damaged might in fact be mended. The room looked *"like a doctors' office but much more exciting,"* Marguerite recalled in *Something About the Author: Autobiography Series (Volume 7)*. *"There were rolls of buckram and cloth-tape in muted shades of green and brown and maroon. There was an enormous jar of delicious-smelling paste with a paintbrush for swabbing it on...."* she wrote. Marguerite was as entranced as she was relieved. The injured book could be repaired, and Marguerite could continue to borrow from the library.

In fact, Marguerite could be much more than a librarian patron. Ovitz offered the thoroughly repentant Marguerite a job mending books on weekday afternoons after school and on Saturdays too. (Marguerite's declared goal of her book-mending job was to save enough money to buy a *"ranchful of horses"*—although she didn't mention how much her book-mending paid.)

Marguerite took to the work with great alacrity and was well-suited to the job—until her dreaminess once more took hold. Marguerite began reading the books as often as she was mending them, and sometimes she read more books than she mended, which made Ovitz furious—so furious, in fact, she decided to fire Marguerite. But when Marguerite shared a passage from a book she was reading (*Summit of the Years* by John Burroughs) with Ovitz, all was forgiven. It seemed that Ovitz was a fan of the great naturalist too, so Marguerite was allowed to keep her job and she and the librarian often shared their thoughts on the Burroughs book.

Published in 1913, *Summit of the Years* is the author's account of what he thought had been his greatest accomplishments in life. It's a weighty tome for a young girl, but Burroughs's emphasis on the importance of nature appealed to Marguerite. *"... that which has interested me most in life, nature, can be seen from lanes and by-paths better even than the turnpike,"* Burroughs wrote. It was just how Marguerite saw the world.

Marguerite later described her love of both libraries and Burroughs (to whom she remained devoted) in an article titled "Those Who Carry Umbrellas" for the *Book Bulletin* of the Chicago Public Library (September 1956), adapted from an earlier talk she had given. *"In a library I have no feeling of solitariness. All about me other people are braiding together little strands of information, too.... In the words of my beloved John Burroughs: 'We have come here to find ourselves. It is so easy to get lost in the world.'"* The title of Marguerite's essay came from a proverb that Marguerite said had informed her life, which read: *"Those who carry umbrellas cannot see the rainbow."*

After graduating from high school, Marguerite remained close to home, enrolling at Milwaukee (Wisconsin) State Normal School (now University of Wisconsin-Milwaukee) with the intention of becoming a teacher—a common ambition for young unmarried women of her generation. The college was conveniently close to her parents' house on the city's east side. Marguerite recalled walking the mile from home to her university classes, sometimes wearing two layers of stockings, not for the warmth but to "fatten" her legs, which she considered too thin to be attractive.

Marguerite described herself as *"very skinny and very homely"* as a teenager and young woman, and she wasn't—by her own admission—particularly popular with boys, who referred to her as "that tall drink of water." It seems like a tame sobriquet by today's standards, but the words still stung. Nevertheless, by the time Marguerite was ready for college, she had become an attractive and poised young woman. In her yearbook photo she wears stylishly poofy bangs, a pearl necklace, and a confident smile. She was an active, engaged student. Marguerite aka "Marge" majored in journalism and was the vice president of the Dramatic Club, as well as a member of the French Club, and president of the Pythia Club. She wrote poetry and plays, and at one point entertained the idea of becoming an actress. Marguerite certainly never lacked dramatic flair, and she would put her talents to good use many years later in the sales and marketing of her books.

A Fated Meeting at a Fishing Camp

The summer after her second year at college, Marguerite's life changed forever—for both better and worse. Her beloved father became deathly ill, and Marguerite met her future husband, Sidney Crocker Henry, at a fishing camp in northern Wisconsin. Sidney (Sid) was on vacation with his family, all of whom were avowed fishermen, and Marguerite was a companion to her sisters Elsie and Gertrude and their respective husband and boyfriend on their trip to the same place.

This "fishing camp" where Marguerite fell in love with her future husband was much more than a camp. In fact, to call Dr. Huber's "Woodland" on Lake Kawaguesaga a fishing camp was a misnomer. It was no mere rustic retreat but a first-rate resort on a seven-hundred-acre lake widely regarded as one of the most beautiful in the Minocqua chain. It was a favored destination of well-to-do German-Americans when Marguerite was young. (Today the region is home to a mix of upscale homes, resorts, and rustic seasonal cabins.)

While the main lodge and cottages at Dr. Huber's resort were rustic (they were constructed of logs), the resort was decidedly exclusive, with amenities that included tennis courts, a golf course, and a "farm-to-table" restaurant. *The History of Lincoln, Oneida and Vilas Counties* (1924) of the Wisconsin Historical Society made the fare and its preparations at Dr. Huber's certainly sound appealing: *"The cuisine is particularly attractive, with fresh vegetables and fruits from the management's gardens and orchards, eggs and fowls from the hennery and dairy products from the herd."*

The Breithaupts enjoyed a comfortable vacation, and although Marguerite provided no details about how she felt about fishing, that was clearly beside the point during that pivotal trip when she spent every day with Sid. Marguerite later described their meeting as fated. *"It was almost like a reunion before we had even met!"* she wrote. The couple was almost immediately inseparable, fishing during the day and dancing at night, perhaps to that year's hit song "When My Baby Smiles at Me" by the Ted Lewis Jazz Band.

A photograph of Marguerite and Sid taken that summer shows a well-dressed, attractive young couple. Marguerite smiles happily under her broad-brimmed hat while Sid, walking slightly in front of Marguerite, has a less exuberant, more guarded expression. But he's holding tight to her hand.

When their vacations ended, Sid wasn't ready to say goodbye, so he invited Marguerite's group to visit his family at their home in Sheboygan. Located on the western edge of Lake Michigan, Sheboygan was a small but quite prosperous town a few hours' drive from Milwaukee. The Henrys, like the Breithaupts, were also well-to-do and also from German stock; Sid Henry's father was born in Germany and emigrated to the United States as a young man, first to Nebraska, where Sid was born, and later moving to Wisconsin and a spacious Victorian home just blocks from the lake. (Sid's father apparently amassed a small fortune.)

Although Marguerite and Sid's families made plans to meet at the fishing camp the following year, smitten Sid wasn't willing to wait. Instead, he came calling for Marguerite at home in Milwaukee soon after the visit to Sheboygan.

Sid was determined to meet Marguerite's parents, particularly Marguerite's father, whom he knew Marguerite revered and whom he knew was quite ill. Marguerite later likened their meeting to the act of Olympic runners passing a torch—the torch, of course, being herself. As it turned out, Marguerite's father died soon after, but Sid kept the torch burning the rest of his life.

Sid, born in 1894, was quite a few years Marguerite's senior and already well-established in his career as a sales manager for a battery company at the time of their marriage. Sid was twenty-eight and Marguerite had just turned twenty-one a month before they were wed. The wedding was described in exquisite detail in the *Sheboygan Press-Telegram*. On May 5, 1923, the headline read: *"Brilliant Wedding of Sidney C. Henry and Miss Breithaupt."* Marguerite's gown was noted as made of white georgette crepe with panels of beaded crystal while her sister Gertrude was attired in pink and silver "changeable taffeta" or shot silk in her role as maid of honor. (A week earlier, the *Milwaukee Journal* ran an announcement of their wedding with an accompanying portrait of Marguerite. Resplendent in a dark dress with a cut-out shoulder and a bejeweled headband, Marguerite was positioned between two young women with similar haircuts, one a bit older. She was identified as Mrs. Raymond L. Maas, *"whose husband has been making attractive pastel portraits of famous folk."*)

Both Sid's and Marguerite's mothers wore black to the wedding—Marguerite's mother attired in black lace and Sid's mother in black georgette. A party followed at the new Hotel Astor in downtown Milwaukee (quite swank at the time, now much less so); then the couple took "a honeymoon in the East" and afterward moved to a small apartment in Chicago.

Sid traveled a great deal in those early years, and Marguerite's mother wasn't a great fan of this fact nor of his profession. She even warned Marguerite of the perils of marrying a traveling man: "Once a traveler, always a traveler," her mother said. While her mother may have intended this as a warning, Marguerite saw it more like a promise of excitement and freedom. A man constantly on the move was exactly the right sort for Marguerite, who loved nothing more than traveling, preferably while chasing down a good story.

In the early years of their marriage, Sid and Marguerite moved several times—from a small apartment on Sheridan Road in Chicago to an apartment in St. Louis where they lived but briefly, and then to several small towns in Illinois, west of Chicago. The first of these towns was Freeport, where they lived for a few years before moving to Naperville and finally to Wayne, their place of residence for over three decades.

During those nomadic years Sid was busy with his sales career, and later managing his several hardware stores, but he was always unfailingly encouraging of Marguerite's writerly ambitions. Sid even suggested the magazines where he thought Marguerite might be able to sell a story. Some of the magazines Sid suggested seemed rather ambitious for a writer who was just starting out, including the most important magazine of the day, *The Saturday Evening Post*. But Sid didn't seem to think that a fledging writer like Marguerite should aim a bit lower; to him, Marguerite belonged in those pages as much as anyone else.

Marguerite's work did appear in *The Saturday Evening Post,* in addition to other magazines and quite a few business journals. In the early years of her marriage, Marguerite was focused on writing features and reporting business news; it would be some time before she would try to publish her first children's book.

Among the pieces she wrote for the *Post* was a series entitled "Turning Points in the Lives of Famous Men," which included a profile of

Archer Wall Douglas, a successful business executive who was also an amateur graphologist. Douglas was small in physical stature, and Marguerite comically described him as *"a little cricket of a man so fragile he had to bind up his legs to walk."* (This wasn't in her *Saturday Evening Post* profile but in an essay she wrote years afterward.)

Douglas's claim to fame was that he could analyze the handwriting of a job applicant and determine whether he or she would be a good fit to a particular position. Over the course of her interview with him, Douglas offered to assess Marguerite's handwriting, which Marguerite eagerly accepted since he offered the analysis for free. But the result of Douglas's evaluation would likely have been greatly discouraging to someone less determined than Marguerite. With the words *"branded into my memory like a sizzling iron,"* recalled Marguerite, Douglas delivered a damning estimation: *"Remember always that you are utterly without imagination,"* he said and even repeated the word "utterly" in order to make his point.

Clearly the cricket-like Douglas wasn't always right.

A sample of Douglas's reasoning was found in a 1924 article in *The Atlantic* entitled "The Art and Nature of Graphology." Douglas described what he found in a writing sample at great—even ponderous—length. Was it perhaps his verbosity that convinced the people who employed him that he was right? *"Capital letters tell of the possession of imagination, or of its absence, they also tell of that fancy which so many mistake for the creative instinct. This is shown by a lack of originality and beauty in the capitals and is most often found in the signatures of women. It tells of daydreams, of things which we vainly believe that we could accomplish, had we only opportunity, and it is as much a matter of temperament as of mentality; moreover, it is something that the writers are usually very shy of confessing. They seem loath to have their fond fancies dragged into the light of day."*

letters

Marguerite clearly wasn't deterred by the graphologist's pessimistic pronouncement of her creative capabilities—some years later she even good-naturedly suggested that Douglas had been right since her success as a children's author came when she told stories based on real life and not fiction. *"He was right! I knew he was right, and I took his advice to heart—which explains why all my stories are based on F-A-C-T,"* she wrote in the essay "A Weft of Truth and a Warp of Fiction," which appeared in *Elementary English,* published by the National Council of Teachers of English.

While Marguerite had succeeded as a precocious eleven-year-old writer and flourished later as a freelancer, it turned out to be much harder to get her first children's book published. In fact, it didn't happen until Marguerite was a middle-aged woman, almost forty years old. The book "went from one publisher to another," Marguerite recalled in a typed piece that reads like a radio transcript entitled "Twenty Questions and Answers," without delving too deeply into what must have been a most frustrating time for the aspiring author.

Marguerite re-wrote that first book—*Geraldine Belinda*—many, many times before it was finally published (she actually had two other books published before *Geraldine Belinda* made it into print). *Geraldine Belinda* was Marguerite's first collaboration with an illustrator, and it would become the model for the rest of her work, and the rest of her professional life. The process and result made her realize that she needed the work of a talented artist to bring her words to life, and she would come to value the illustrators of her books so much that several of them became her good friends. One, a wildly charismatic, talented artist named Wesley Dennis, would develop into a dear friend indeed.

First Collaborations

Her partner in the creation of *Geraldine Belinda* was the artist Gladys Rourke-Blackwood, a well-known children's book illustrator of the day. (Rourke-Blackwood has even been credited with the creation of paper dolls in book form, although sadly she didn't get rich off her brilliant idea.) At the time, Marguerite and Sid lived in a modest rental house, which Marguerite described as "scooped out of a ravine," that was conveniently close to Rourke-Blackwood's "charming Hansel and Gretel cottage" in Freeport, Illinois, and both women had lived in Chicago before moving to the smaller town.

A small city some hundred or so miles west of Chicago, Freeport was nicknamed "Pretzel City" in a nod to its German founders, and its claim to fame was the fact it was the location of the second presidential debate between Abraham Lincoln and Stephen Douglas in 1858. (A town statue commemorates the occasion.) Freeport was also the home of one of the earliest libraries built by American steel magnate and philanthropist Andrew Carnegie—a fact which surely must have appealed to bibliophile like Marguerite.

Rourke-Blackwood and her husband Merl Blackwood (who was also an artist) had moved to Freeport after he had been hired as an art teacher in the Freeport schools. Rourke-Blackwood, a few years Marguerite's junior, had also been sickly as a child, although unlike Marguerite, she had a visible handicap—her right hand wasn't properly formed so she had to train herself to work with her left hand, which was no small feat for an artist. Rourke-Blackwood kept her right hand so well-hidden in the pocket of her smock that it was much later in their friendship before Marguerite would see it. Marguerite even commented how Rourke-Blackwood had attended a party with her hand tucked in a white fur muff, which Marguerite found incredibly stylish, not realizing the accessory's true purpose.

Although both women were childless, they shared a keen interest in creating children's books and ended up collaborating on two others after *Geraldine Belinda*: *Auno and Tauno* and *Dilly Dally Sally*. Marguerite recalled meetings with Rourke-Blackwood fondly, often as not conducted over cups of hot cocoa at the Blackwood kitchen table. Visiting the Blackwood house was an *"Event,"* recalled Marguerite (capitalizing the word to show its importance). *"From the very beginning our collaborations became the most exciting, all-consuming thing in our lives."*

The two women were at similar points in their careers. Both were modestly successful—Marguerite was a working writer and

Blackwood was a working artist, but neither had yet produced a book. Since they lived less than a mile apart, they could visit quite often to trade proposals and plans. It was the kind of close connection and exchange of ideas that Marguerite came to prize most of all—and that kept her from feeling too lonely during Sid's frequent absences when he traveled for work.

Sometimes Marguerite sought a different sort of company when she worked. When she sat for an interview with Elisabeth Yager of the *Freeport Journal-Standard*, Marguerite told Yager that she had written much of *Geraldine Belinda* in *"the peaceful quiet of the old Lincoln Boulevard cemetery"* of Freeport because she didn't want anyone to see her struggle with writing her book. Was this tidbit true or just a dramatic idea that the theatrical Marguerite had dreamed up? Certainly, writing a book in the middle of a cemetery sounded more interesting than writing one while sitting alone at her desk at home.

The interviewer—whom Marguerite had clearly captivated—didn't query her subject further on this point but instead noted Marguerite's appearance in favorable terms. Like many who profiled Marguerite over the years, Yager remarked not only on Marguerite's impeccable attire but her seeming youthfulness. Although Marguerite was forty-six years old at the time of the interview, Yager described the writer as *"an extremely attractive young matron who was given to blushing— and who resisted talking about herself."* Yager was apparently so captivated by Marguerite's modesty that she mentioned it more than once, noting that Marguerite was far more voluble when talking with children and writing amusing notes for them when she signed their books.

Marguerite later rather self-deprecatingly described *Geraldine Belinda* as a book whose character was not unlike her childhood self, a *"snippety, selfish little brat."* She liked the idea of writing a book entirely in verse, and an unpublished version of *Geraldine Belinda* was written entirely in rhyme: *Geraldine Belinda Marybelle Scott/Buttoned her coat and set off at a trot/Her pigtails danced as she flew down the street/And the tassels on her shoes kept time with her feet.* Sadly, as much as Marguerite and Rourke-Blackwood loved the result, the editor at Viking Press, the redoubtable May Massee, did not.

Massee, a highly regarded editor of children's books (and fellow Milwaukee native) felt that while children might enjoy the rhyming, an adult would not. It would grow tiresome when reading the book aloud, Massee thought. Massee's recommendations appear to have held sway, as no rhymes appear in the published work.

Interestingly, Massee was not only the editor who had published the perennial bestseller *The Story of Ferdinand* (1936) but also found and fostered the talent of Ludwig Bemelmans, the author of the *Madeline* books whose rhymes became famous (*they left the house at half past nine/in two straight lines*). The first of the *Madeline* books was published in 1939, three years before *Geraldine Belinda*—had Massee perhaps grown tired of rhyming books for children, or did she simply dislike Marguerite's rhyme scheme? Whatever the reason, it seemed to dissuade Marguerite from employing the technique ever again; she never wrote another rhyming book, although she and Rourke-Blackwood both continued to love their first rendition of *Geraldine Belinda*. *"Gladys and I preferred the rhymed version by far and to this day we break into it on the slightest provocation,"* Marguerite wrote.

This didn't, however, mean that Marguerite thought her partiality for the rhyme was right; she had enormous respect for Massee—so much so that when Massee died in 1970, Marguerite wrote a heartfelt tribute to the editor who she credited with bringing she and Wesley Dennis, the artist she would work with on what would be her most successful and best-known books, to their *"close working relationship."* Furthermore, Marguerite added, she regularly sought Massee's advice. *"She didn't mind at all my discussing a knotty problem in a story, or in life, with her. It became at once her problem, and she helped thrash it out."* And when Massee rejected her very first effort, Massee responded (*"with beautiful simplicity,"* noted Marguerite) that the effort *"lacks guts."* Marguerite took her words to heart, writing, *"That has been my test of a book ever since."*

While Marguerite created *Geraldine Belinda* with her own childish self as a model, a Finnish couple named Beda and Effendi Walkeala inspired the next book she wrote, *Auno and Tauno: A Story of Finland.* The Walkealas worked for the Henrys during their Freeport years. Beda did all the cooking and cleaning since (by her own admission) Marguerite wasn't much of a cook. Beda's husband Effendi took care of the Henrys' lawn. The couple told Marguerite stories of their childhood in Finland as they worked, and Marguerite diligently copied them down. *Auno and Tauno* was dedicated to them: *"Their recent memories of Finland are captured between the covers of this book."*

Auno and Tauno was published in 1940—before *Geraldine Belinda,* despite being written after—by Albert Whitman & Company, the Chicago-based children's book publisher. A sweet and charming book with rather simple illustrations by Rourke-Blackwood, *Auno and Tauno* was well-received by the critics. It's a much slighter work than Marguerite's later books. Nothing much happens to either Auno or Tauno—they go to school, have a few small adventures and misadventures on their way home. But the setting in Finland makes them memorable, and Marguerite sprinkled Finnish words and phrases throughout the book. (She was clearly taken with the language, and the foreign words also helped fill the story out.) Perhaps most importantly, the book reveals the beginnings of Marguerite's writerly voice: gentle, reassuring, and slightly bemused.

Readers of *Auno and Tauno* learned that *tupa* is the Finnish word for the main room of the house and that *kantele* is a kind of Finnish harp. Marguerite captured the mood and the feel of Finland in winter when *the days are gray like kitten's fluff* and the feeling of riding in the sleigh behind Tapio the horse: *"It seemed as if the sleigh were headed for the Northern Lights and would soon be tangled in the red streamers blazing across the sky,"* thinks Tauno, aka "Little Cuckoo." Tapio, a gray horse, is depicted with an oddly blank expression, and in one illustration he has a flaxen mane and in another it is gray. He is the first of the many, many horses that would appear in Marguerite's books, if perhaps one of the least memorable or accurate artistically.

Rourke-Blackwood was given the lesser credit of "pictures by" on the cover of both *Auno and Tauno* and *Geraldine Belinda*—never mind that these early books, and every book that followed, revealed that Marguerite's words, however well-chosen, needed the work of a talented artist to bring her stories to life. But the two women remained friends, both during their artistic collaboration and long after it ended, exchanging letters and holiday cards after Marguerite and Sid moved away from Freeport. In a 1979 letter to Marguerite, who was by then living on the West Coast, Rourke-Blackwood noted that her niece in San Clemente, California, had sent her a clipping from *The Los Angeles Times* that featured a profile of Marguerite. *"I thought they gave you a great write-up and I am happy to be part of it. Thrilled to see my name in print again. Thank you!"* Rourke-Blackwood wrote.

Marguerite had a singular talent for friendship, and she and Sid maintained ties with other Freeport residents long after they moved away. The local Freeport paper often reported on their doings and their whereabouts when they were living elsewhere but spending time with Freeport friends. A 1959 notice in the *Freeport Journal-Standard* took note of the fact that resident Leonard C. Ferguson and his wife vacationed with *"Mr. and Mrs. Sidney Henry"* in the Virgin Islands. The paper also noted that *"Mrs. Henry"* had *"won some awards"* for her books and her husband was *"formerly associated with Burgess Battery and is now with Ben Franklin stores."* Although Marguerite was on her way to becoming a famous author by then, Marguerite's and Sid's professional credentials were accorded equal weight.

A New Illustrator

While Rourke-Blackwood possessed a charming style, she wasn't a particularly gifted equine artist. Marguerite's next co-author and illustrator, the talented Diana Thorne, was tremendously gifted at drawing just about everything, but especially animals, and she was with few peers when it came to capturing the expression and essence of dogs.

At the time of their meeting, Thorne was better known and more accomplished than Marguerite, and her work was much sought-after by the rich and famous. She had even been commissioned to draw President Franklin D. Roosevelt's Scottish Terrier Fala, who was, at that time, the most-photographed dog in America.

Diana Thorne (also known as Diana North) was born Ann Woursell in what was then Russia (now Ukraine) and grew up in western Canada in a large family like Marguerite's, although unlike Marguerite, she was the oldest rather than youngest child. Her family left Canada for Germany, and when World War I began, they moved again, this time to England. By 1920, Woursell had moved to New York.

Woursell transformed herself into Diana Thorne sometime early in her professional life, and it isn't entirely clear when or why she changed her name. (There was no "Mr. Thorne.") She was a beautiful, stylish woman in her youth. She and Marguerite only collaborated on two books: *A Boy and A Dog* and *The Little Fellow*, published in 1944 and 1945 respectively. The name Diana Thorne is allotted top billing on the book covers above Marguerite's—*Drawings by Diana Thorne/ Story by Marguerite Henry*—presumably because hers was then the more famous name.

The Little Fellow of the second book's title is a small, sweet colt named Chip, and the story unfolds through Chip's eyes as he takes measure of his world, which is chiefly composed of his mother Chocolate and the few people around him. Chip is a frolicsome and rather aggressive youngster, and his pushiness gets him into trouble with another colt named Strawberry Jenks. The story is charming if a bit slight, but some parts, especially the dialogue, are by today's standards decidedly cringe-making. The descriptions of the stable boy Whitey who is Black are unfortunate, to say the least. Whitey is *"exactly the same color as Chocolate but still everyone called him Whitey,"* Marguerite wrote.

Whitey's face is *"shiny"* and he talks in cartoonish, buffoonish words. *"Lan sakes! Dat foal of yo's is growing jes lak a weed. Fack is, he's mos nigh growed up. An' a thorobred ef I evah seed one! De white folks gwine be mighty proud o' yo' baby,"* Marguerite wrote in the voice of Whitey. On the opposite page is a drawing of a grinning Black boy. Many years later (1975) Marguerite chose to rewrite the entire book, changing the dialogue and even the race of Whitey (from Black to white), and the illustrations of Rich Rudish replaced those of Diana Thorne. (His artwork was accomplished but lacks the poignant expression of Thorne's.) Marguerite was sensitive to the fact that the original book—considered acceptable forty years earlier—was construed as racist, and for that reason, she did not wish that edition to continue to be sold. (While some copies of the original can be found on websites such as eBay, the revised edition is the one most frequently seen today.)

Reviews of the original version of the book were favorable ("*a happy little picture book*"), particularly regarding the illustrations. A review in *The New York Herald Tribune Weekly Book Review* dated May 20, 1945, noted: "*The pictures have not only charm but distinction; color excellently reproduced has so much to do with that reproduction in black and white would not do them justice.*" Interestingly there was no mention of the words.

Thorne kept studios in both Chicago and New York. She had at least one male companion, and she may or may not have been married to fellow artist and illustrator Carton Moore-Park, whom she identified at various points in their years together as her husband. While Thorne might have enjoyed greater fame than Marguerite during their partnership, her life proved far less stable and much less happy. When Moore-Park died, Thorne was forced to scramble for work, and as her commissions from wealthy patrons dried up, she was reduced to begging friends and relations for money. By 1962 she had been diagnosed with mental illness and was confined to Bellevue Hospital, the New York public hospital for the poor. She died the following year and is said to be buried on Hart Island, where the destitute and the homeless of New York are interred. It was a sad coda to the brilliant artist who set the stage for the Marguerite's next illustrator and co-creator.

The Birth of a Profound Partnership

It is no overstatement to say that Wesley Dennis was the single most consequential person to enter Marguerite's life, save for her husband Sid. Born on Cape Cod, Massachusetts, in 1903, Dennis drew horses from a young age, as did his brother Morgan, who was the far more successful artist in their early years, although Wesley Dennis later earned far greater acclaim.

Dennis was the artist whose work was so singular, his sensibilities and his love and knowledge of horses so great and so close to Marguerite's own (he knew a great deal more about horses than she), that Marguerite shared book royalties with him equally. This was a remarkable, nearly unheard-of arrangement in publishing circles, but Dennis would become so integral to her work and to her life that Marguerite not only made him her full artistic partner but her promotional partner, as well, and they traveled the country together on book signings and tours. When Dennis died of a heart attack at sixty-three years of age (coincidentally, the same age as her father), Marguerite wrote to friends and family, and later her readers, that she considered never writing again.

In the years before Marguerite and Dennis met, Dennis was working at a racetrack near Boston to be around horses and to better understand what they looked like and how they moved. Of course, Dennis hoped to sell a few paintings of the racehorses at the track to their owners, as well, although he was not a mere horse portraitist but a serious artist who had spent time studying in Paris some years before.

As mentioned, Dennis and Marguerite met thanks, in a roundabout way, to the redoubtable May Massee. Dennis was traveling on vacation in New Mexico when Massee reached out to him. She was so impressed with the work that she'd seen of his that she commissioned Dennis to illustrate (and write) his first book. That book, *Flip*, published in 1941 by Viking Press, told the story of a young colt who wants to jump over a stream, and it was the one that Marguerite discovered while she was searching for an illustrator for a manuscript she'd just written, which she was calling "Justin Morgan Had a Horse." Marguerite had been immediately captivated by the charming illustrations of the winsome colt with the star in the middle of his forehead and decided that Dennis simply had to be the one to illustrate her new book. (Marguerite later jokingly remarked that part of her decision to pursue Dennis was because all the other great equine artists whose work she admired were long dead.)

Marguerite was initially daunted by the fact that Dennis (then) lived in New York, far from her home in Illinois. It seemed too great a gamble to travel all the way to New York just to chat with a prospective illustrator, but Sid urged Marguerite to plan the meeting. If Marguerite felt as strongly as she did about his work, then surely Dennis was the right artist for her book, he reasoned. Marguerite simply had to travel to the East Coast. It was one of the many consequential decisions that Sid made that helped further Marguerite's career.

Marguerite had mailed Dennis a manuscript of the book in question some time before they met. She already had a publisher for it, but she was nervous as to what Dennis might think; this was her first full-length children's book. Marguerite and Dennis had agreed that their meeting would take place in a "writing room" of the Barbizon Hotel on the Upper East Side of Manhattan. The Barbizon Hotel, on East 63rd Street, had been designed as a hotel specifically for professional women—aspiring secretaries, models, and actresses. It was dubbed "The Dollhouse" for its seemingly endless array of beautiful, desirable, single ladies, and quite a few (later) famous actresses made it their home. It was said that J.D. Salinger, author of *The Catcher in the Rye*, hung out in the coffee shop located in the hotel in hopes of picking up women—before he became a famous recluse.

Marguerite recalled the exact time—2:30 p.m.—of that momentous first 1941 meeting with Dennis and described their encounter in a suitably dramatic fashion, which was remarkably reminiscent of her recollection of her first meeting with Sid. In Marguerite's telling, she and Dennis both experienced a sort of *coup de foudre* that afternoon, although it was presumably purely professional—a recognition of fellow feeling between writer and artist. And while their connection wasn't romantic, it was an enduring love that lasted until Dennis's death.

Marguerite set the scene of the encounter when retelling the story in *The Illustrated Marguerite Henry* (Checkerboard Press, 1980) as if she was writing one of her college-era plays. She wrote that she had been *"like a cat waiting to snap up a mouse"* at the door of the Barbizon writing room, and exactly at the prescribed hour, *"a big shaggy St. Bernard sort of person wearing a Sherlock Holmes hat burst in."*

Dennis was a year younger than Marguerite, and he was not only quite handsome and charismatic but also quite self-assured—her temperamental opposite in every regard. Marguerite was temperate, reflective, gentle, and quiet whereas Dennis was flamboyant and extravagant. (Dennis was also, by all accounts, a chain-smoker and a heavy drinker—other ways in which he and Marguerite differed.) Marguerite was soon captivated as much by the man as his art.

The way that Dennis worked enthralled and astonished her as well. It wasn't just the quality of his artwork but the speed with which he accomplished it that impressed so much. *"Many times he [Dennis] had his pictures for a chapter all done before my final text,"* Marguerite recalled. She described their differences—fittingly, if self-deprecatingly—in equine terms: Dennis was the *"Thoroughbred built for speed"* and she was merely *"a workhorse."*

Dennis had read the manuscript of "Justin Morgan," and he was keen to collaborate with Marguerite— although "keen" was probably too mild a term to describe how Dennis told Marguerite he felt about her book. Dennis wanted to illustrate the book so badly he didn't care about money, he said. Marguerite recounted Dennis's exact (and to her, quite thrilling) words: *"I'm crazy to do the book. And I don't care whether I get paid for it or not."* It was a suitably cinematic beginning to their hugely successful collaboration and friendship.

While their mutual appreciation was instantaneous and unabated, their work habits differed as dramatically as their temperaments. Dennis liked to be outside, preferably in a barn or a field surrounded by animals, while he was sketching. *("I have a studio in the middle of a paddock," he said.)* Marguerite's favorite writing location was at a library or at her desk with a dog underfoot (the story she told of writing parts of *Geraldine Belinda* in a cemetery was a one-off). Marguerite often said that she wrote best when she had someone nearby—just as she had when she was a child.

While Marguerite was childless, Dennis had two sons named Reid and Morgan with his second wife, Dorothy Schiller Boggs. Before her, Dennis had been married very briefly to a young widow named Olive Emma Jenkins Garland from Buzzards Bay, Massachusetts, who had two sons of her own and to whom Dennis remained close—he even rented a studio in Buzzards Bay from one of them. Dennis had met Schiller Boggs five years after he and Garland were divorced, while playing polo in Massachusetts. Schiller Boggs attended the game; the two were married several years later in 1940.

Dennis and his family were living in New York when he and Marguerite met. (They lived for a time in a farmhouse in the Hudson Valley region owned by his and Marguerite's editor, May Massee. The nine-room stone house, located outside the village of Montgomery, New York, was next door to the Hungarian-born Kate Seredy's farm—another Massee author, illustrator, and friend who won the Newbery medal for her book *The White Stag*, published by Viking in 1937.) The Dennis family later moved to a sprawling mountaintop farm (one hundred and twenty acres) in Warrenton, Virginia, named Chatterbox Farms. It was, by all accounts, a paradise for both people and animals. There, Dennis kept horses and ponies and all sorts of creatures, including dogs, geese, and even a crow named Charlie, who eventually starred in a book that Dennis wrote entitled *A Crow I Know*. Both Dennises were also regulars at the local fox hunting meets, riding more for fun than competitively.

While Marguerite was a horse lover, by all accounts it was Dennis who was the true horseman. He lived and breathed horses every day. His was the life that the child Marguerite had dreamt of leading one day.

letters

WEATHER ~Fine~ ~File~

THE UNIVERSITY OF VERMONT
BURLINGTON, VERMONT

The Billings Library
Office of the Librarian

March 6, 1943

Miss Marguerite Henry
Naperville, Illinois

Dear Miss Henry:

I have looked through the newspapers in which the account of the President's trip was given, and I am sorry to say that I find no mention of the weather on that day. ~Neither do I find that there is any reference to the fact that Mr. Monroe mounted the horse named Justin Morgan during the parade and made some comment about him.~

Enclosed is a copy of the speech made by the President. I hope it will give you some useful information.

Very truly yours,

Helen B Shattuck

Helen B. Shattuck
Librarian

HBS:MD
Enc.

weather on that day

[Since there is no mention given I should expect that it was a fair day] H.B.S.

JUSTIN MORGAN
HAD A HORSE

3

*"This is the story of a common, ordinary little work horse
which turned out to be the father
of a famous family of American horses."*

—

FROM *JUSTIN MORGAN HAD A HORSE*
(FIRST PUBLISHED 1945)

S ince Marguerite had already written *Justin Morgan Had a Horse* before she and Wesley Dennis met, his illustrations—theoretically, at least—had to match Marguerite's prose. But their work was immediately collaborative, establishing a pattern for the eleven subsequent books that would bear both their names. Dennis would mail Marguerite some sketches for her comments, and she'd offer her thoughts in return. For example, when Dennis sent Marguerite a preliminary drawing of Little Bub aka Figure aka Justin Morgan—the main horse character in *Justin Morgan Had a Horse*—Marguerite asked Dennis if he could draw Little Bub, and his horse friend Ebenezer, a bit differently. *"Could the little Morgan show his frisky, fiery spirits in contrast to the older, calmer colt?"* she asked. Dennis never questioned whether she was right. Instead, he quickly responded with a pitch-perfect illustration of the two colts, one led sedately by schoolmaster Justin Morgan (for whom the colt Little Bub was later named) and the wilder colt lowering his head to buck, his hindquarters pointed toward the young schoolboy Joel, who doesn't even seem to notice.

Marguerite was not the only one in the partnership who felt comfortable offering an opinion or direction. Dennis would often suggest a place in a manuscript to Marguerite where he thought an illustration might be appropriate. He was not just an illustrator but a careful, nuanced reader as well. For Dennis, as well as Marguerite, the words and the pictures had to match.

Spinning Fact and Fiction

The name "Little Bub," bestowed on Marguerite's fictional horse character Justin Morgan, was one of Marguerite's many fanciful notions—a name she conjured up without any actual evidence that the real Justin Morgan (the horse credited with the creation of the Morgan horse breed as its "foundation stallion") was given such a moniker. But Marguerite liked the way it sounded, and she had solid reasons for naming him such, as she later explained to a young reader named Sandy who wrote to ask Marguerite how the name Little Bub came about.

It seemed that Sandy was quite well informed about the Morgan breed, and he had additional questions for Marguerite on that subject as well: Was Justin Morgan the same horse that was also named Figure? And if so, which name was correct? (Marguerite's readers might have tended toward young, but they were remarkably well-informed about horses and history and acted like a self-appointed army of fact checkers, often questioning the accuracy of a particular setting or time or animal description.)

Marguerite's reply to Sandy was a characteristically charming combination of fact and fantasy and revealed a bit about how she put the story of Justin Morgan—and so many of her other books—together. The name "Bub" was a bit of whimsy, Marguerite conceded, but it was whimsy based on fact. As Marguerite explained to her young correspondent: *"Bub is a nickname often used in New England in pioneer days so it seems logical to me that Joel might have given his colt a pet name like Little Bub."*

Furthermore, Marguerite added, the name Figure didn't seem to fit such a strapping colt. And as Wesley's illustrations revealed, that was a very good point. Marguerite's telling of how Figure then acquired the name of the schoolmaster who once owned him (Justin Morgan) is a bit fanciful too: *"No one knew quite how it happened, but after Justin Morgan died his full name was given to the little horse,"* Marguerite wrote in the opening of chapter fourteen of the book.

In Marguerite's fictionalized telling, the horse Justin Morgan, now known by the schoolmaster's name, is put up for sale. The character of the schoolboy Joel, now grown, hears the news that the horse he knew as a spirited young colt and called Little Bub will be sold in front of the sheriff's office in Randolph, Vermont. When the man who tells Joel the news doesn't appear to understand why Joel cares so much, Joel's answer is equal parts determination and heartbreak: *"'Twas me who gentled him. And 'tis me who wants to buy him."* He has five silver dollars. It isn't enough.

Marguerite wrote of Joel's pining for Little Bub as a child might pine for a beloved pony—as she herself had for many years. *"O please let him be safe. Let him be well. Let him live long enough for me to find him again,"* Joel prays in the book. All the words are fiction but also part of a timeless truth—a human's love for a horse.

The schoolmaster Justin Morgan did actually exist, but the character of Joel, fashioned to be a pupil and friend of his former schoolmaster, was Marguerite's idea—he was simply the protagonist she needed to bring the story of the foundational sire of the Morgan Horse breed to life. And there were some supporting facts to bolster her idea: Joel Goss did truly exist, and he did buy the horse that would become known as the first Morgan when the stallion was quite old (in 1816). Marguerite decided that the only possible reason a man of limited means might have to buy such an old broken-down horse was because the man had loved the horse as a boy, long ago.

As Marguerite described in her newsletter to fans, when she was researching *Justin Morgan Had a Horse*, she had written to the librarian of Claremont, New Hampshire, to determine if there was, in fact, a record of a man named Joel Goss. It turned out there was, and there was also a living relative of his, the then-eighty-eight-year-old Miss Fannie Goss, who was living in Claremont and who happened to be his granddaughter. Fannie Goss confirmed to Marguerite that her grandfather did, in fact, exist at the same time as the schoolmaster Justin Morgan, though there was no proof they knew one another. But since it was possible, Marguerite decided she would provide the connection. As Marguerite's story went, the schoolmaster Justin Morgan took a long trip to collect a debt, and the result was bringing home two horses—one of which was Little Bub. In reimagining this event for her book, Marguerite thought Master Morgan would have to have done this along with someone else—and that person could easily have been Joel Goss. It was creative conjuring blended with diligent research and careful incorporation of historically accurate facts—a method of writing that Marguerite went on to practice over and over in book after book to great effect. (Marguerite's initial source for the story of Justin Morgan and the two colts was an old Vermonter named

David Dana Hewitt.) The stories that Marguerite conjured resonated deeply because they were filled with emotion and framed in truth.

One of Marguerite's great strengths as a writer was the fact she was an inveterate researcher and taker of notes on subjects, large and small. Her notes for *Justin Morgan,* invariably in pencil, often covered both sides of various papers, including hotel stationary and bills from Sid's business. Marguerite also made special use of manila folders—lots and lots of manila folders that contained all sorts of factual snippets gleaned through her research that she would later decide to use or discard in the writing of the book. *"Horse of all work/All around ride and drive horse/ Trot quick, short, springy"* she wrote about the Morgan breed. Some indicated calculations of distances traveled, given that back in the days of Justin Morgan, distances in the United States were counted in "rods" rather than miles. Marguerite's memo: *"There are 5½ yards in a rod."*

While Marguerite was content to take liberties with some names and places, she was surprisingly exact about certain facts. For example, Marguerite wrote a letter to Helen B. Shattuck, a librarian in Burlington, Vermont, on March 6, 1943, asking about the weather on the day of President James Monroe's visit to the state. Was the day rainy or fair? If Ms. Shattuck was surprised by the exactitude of such an inquiry, she gave no indication. *"I have looked through the newspapers in which the account of the President's trip is given, and I am sorry to say that I find no mention of the weather on that day,"* Ms. Shattuck crisply replied. Interestingly, Ms. Shattuck added a line that Marguerite crossed out: *"Neither do I find that there is any reference to the fact that Mr. Monroe mounted the horse named Justin Morgan during the parade and made some comment about him."*

The latter may or may not have been true; the newspapers of the day noted that the President stepped down from his carriage in Burlington to ride a horse. As Marguerite reasoned, why not have that horse be Justin

Morgan? She'd already decided that President Monroe would meet Justin Morgan. Additionally, for Marguerite's purposes, it would be a sunlit morning when President Monroe appeared in the crucial scene.

In fact, Marguerite wasn't content to just have President Monroe meet the main character of her book; she decided there had to be some dramatic action as well. Thus, as she tells it in the pages of *Justin Morgan Had a Horse,* while the President was riding his own horse through downtown Burlington, his horse was stung by a bee. (Never mind according to the local papers the President was riding in a carriage, not astride.) In Marguerite's version, the President dismounted from his fretting horse and the townspeople clamored for him to ride one of their horses instead. President Monroe scanned the crowd and chose Justin Morgan.

When wild cheers followed a speech from the President, and in the middle of it all, Little Bub gave a little bow, *"It was hard to tell whether the Morgan or the President was the hero of the day!"* Marguerite wrote. As her readers would attest, this may not have been factually accurate, but it certainly felt right.

Interestingly enough, the American Morgan Horse Association includes the ride by President Monroe on their website under "The Life and Times of Figure," giving the date of the ride as July 22, 1817. But two further entries in their timeline are rather somber, and are not included in Marguerite's story: Justin Morgan the horse was sold two years after the ride in Burlington to Levi Bean of Chelsea, Vermont, and he died in 1821 from a kick of another horse. This was the first of many times that Marguerite decided to omit some of the sadder facts of a horse's or a man's real life from one of her books.

Marguerite's research was exhaustive and inevitably included repeated trips to the library and voluminous correspondence with local historians and horsemen, but it also meant traveling to the places where her stories took place—in the case of *Justin Morgan Had a Horse,* it was

Vermont. Indeed, the last pages of the book include acknowledgments of the people and places to whom the author was grateful, followed by two pages of names. It would also be the first of many of her books with an exhaustive bibliography, and it was as much a rarity then as it is now for a children's book to be annotated thus. Among those whom Marguerite credited with research assistance was Walter B. Mahony, the great-great-great grandson of Justin Morgan, as well as Fannie Goss, the granddaughter of Joel Goss. Several libraries and librarians are cited, along with "the late David Dana Hewitt" whom Marguerite labeled "Vermont pioneer." As her many sources reveal, factual accuracy was important to Marguerite—although it was often trumped by an "emotional truth" (this would be apparent perhaps nowhere more vividly than in her next, most famous book, *Misty of Chincoteague*).

Addendum: The Second Version
of *Justin Morgan Had a Horse*

Justin Morgan turned out to be a book that Marguerite would revise substantially several years after its initial publication; in fact, the book grew from a mere ninety pages to nearly twice its original length. The second version also included many more original illustrations and may be the only Newbery honor book to be revised so significantly after publication. (A Newbery "honor" book is one considered to be of merit and distinction—a kind of "runner up" to the ultimate prize, the Newbery Medal, which is awarded annually by the American Library Association, or ALA, "to the author of the most distinguished contribution to American literature for children.")

Marguerite's publisher Rand McNally had asked Marguerite to rewrite the book so it might better fit the format and length of the books that followed *Justin Morgan*, and Marguerite was happy to oblige.

Indeed, Marguerite wasn't the least bit word-proud when it came to her original book and seemed nearly giddy at the prospect of re-entering Justin Morgan's world. The original book was *"only a skeleton glorified by the pictures that Wesley Dennis had done for it. It needed body. And it needed life breathed into it,"* Marguerite wrote. The new edition was published in 1954, and it is the version that most readers know and read today.

With the second *Justin Morgan,* Marguerite decided to dig more deeply into the character and life of Joel Goss. What was his motivation to want the horse? How and when did he become a miller? What did he say and do and how did he feel when the schoolmaster who owned Justin Morgan died? There were many unanswered questions in the original book and many opportunities to research the story more deeply—and of course, enliven the details with Marguerite's own ideas about how it all happened and how the characters felt.

The second edition of the book is filled with even more beautiful illustrations than the first. Unlike many artists, Dennis didn't mind adding extra drawings, Marguerite noted. He would draw as many as they both thought were needed to complement the text—or revise illustrations accordingly. For example, in the second version of the book, both the horses and people look notably different from their original incarnations. They seem to have more personality and ex-pression; somehow Joel Goss looks "happier" too. In some of the original illustrations he seemed to appear cross—perhaps Marguerite noticed that.

There was one particularly interesting change between editions found near the end of the book: the illustration of President Monroe astride Justin Morgan is allotted a two-page spread in the first edition and only a single much smaller page in the second. He is also transformed from a dark-haired man to a white-haired (older?) man, appearing more dignified, more statesmanlike. Justin Morgan has also become a more impressive, solid-looking horse. Were the changes due to new research? There are no further letters from Ms. Shattuck to prove whether these changes were based in fact or something that Marguerite had just decided was right.

The second edition won rave reviews from critics and reviewers. In the "Books and Authors" column in the *Pensacola News-Journal* (October 17, 1954) columnist Michael Leigh opined: *"Only such a perfectionist as Marguerite Henry would attempt a book which had already been judged a runner-up for the Newbery Award in children's literature. But this famous author has rewritten* Justin Morgan Had a Horse *and has made it better than ever."* A review in *The Montgomery Advertiser* (October 24, 1954) hailed it as *"a wonderful story for young people, full of the magic of rural life when this country was young"* and noted its *"exquisite illustrations."*

As a Newbery Medal of Honor book, *Justin Morgan* had not only established Marguerite as a children's author of consequence, but it was also the book that made her fall in love with the Morgan Horse. In fact, when Marguerite finally became a horse owner, late in middle age, her first horse was a Morgan named Friday. Frequently, Marguerite noted the fact of her late-in-life horse ownership to her heartbroken correspondents who wrote of their desire for a horse. *"Never give up—even if you must wait a long time,"* was how she counseled readers. Her gratitude at having waited for, and found, the right horse can be sensed in the dedication of the second edition of *Justin Morgan Had a Horse*: *"To Friday and Fred Tejan who gentled him."*

Welcome to Wayne

When Marguerite wrote the first version of *Justin Morgan*, she and Sid had recently moved to a *"weathered ranch house in a sea of violets,"* as

Marguerite later described their home in Wayne, Illinois. Set far back from busy Wayne Road (now Army Trail Road) behind a large front yard (the very one that became known to her correspondents and fans as "Mole Meadow"), the Henry house was conveniently located near the village train station, where the commuter trains regularly ran to and from Chicago. That was one of Wayne's chief attractions to both Marguerite and Sid, who had begun to acquire several "Ben Franklins" (local five-and-dime/hardware stores.) There was also the fact of his golf club in St. Charles. Sid was a dedicated golfer who spent much of his nonworking life on a golf course.

As a child who grew up in a city, Marguerite often said that she didn't know anything about animals until she and Sid moved to Wayne in 1940. She once told an interviewer for *The Chicago Tribune* (April 11, 1962) that the excitement and joy of her life in Wayne was an opportunity to experience her "delayed childhood," and it was largely thanks to Sid that the dreams of her youth came true in their Wayne years. In photographs of Marguerite and Sid at home in Wayne, Sid is invariably dressed in a suit and tie, every inch the grownup, while Marguerite holds fast to one animal or another, looking very much like the delighted child.

One of the greatest attractions of Wayne for Marguerite was that it was back then, and still is today, a very horse-centric town. In fact, Wayne was designed specifically for horses and riders, thanks to an early visionary named Mark Dunham who bred Percheron horses and created a virtual horse paradise in the mid-nineteenth century. Dunham bought thousands of acres of land that eventually included riding trails and a private rail car that ran to and from Chicago. He even built a large residence called "Dunham Castle," which still stands, down the road from Marguerite's house and just across the street from what would come to be known as "Misty's Meadow"—a patch of grass the pony who inspired *Misty of Chincoteague* may well have crossed during the years she lived in Wayne with Marguerite and Sid (although "Misty's Meadow" did not belong to the Henrys).

While Dunham's holdings had been sold off and his one-time stable had become the home of the Dunham Woods Riding Club, there were still many large horse farms around the Henry house (as there are even today) when Marguerite and Sid arrived in Wayne. Although their property was relatively small—around two acres or so—it was, as Marguerite wrote to one of her fans, a place *"with enough grazing ground to keep a pony happy."* In fact, at one point their property would be home to a pony, a horse, *and* a burro...all cozily stabled in the back yard.

The story of Misty, the pony who lived in that stable in Wayne (adorned with a sign drawn by Dennis that read *"Good keeping for horses,"* which first appeared as an illustration in *Justin Morgan*), would become one of the most-loved children's books of all time, and Wayne, Illinois, would play a large role in the book's success, as Marguerite later described in an essay "Horse Sense is Stable Thinking." *"Everyone who yearns to write a book should be fortunate enough to live in Wayne! Source material is just waiting to be mined in every castle and cottage,"* she wrote. And if not (all) of the material could be mined from Wayne itself, its townspeople were more than happy to become part of a story she told—as Marguerite discovered when she brought that pony named Misty home.

letters

May 28th 1991

Dear Mrs. Henry,

I am so thankful that you could come to our school It was so nice having you. I was so excited when I herd you were coming to our class. I would love to be an auther too. I would love to own Misty

4

MISTY
OF CHINCOTEAGUE

CHAPTER FOUR

4

"Misty seemed to sense the importance of this moment.
She backed away from the group, her head uplifted,
not toward the sea and the island of Assateague, but inland,
toward the well-pounded trails of Chincoteague. Her whole body
quivered as if she saw a promise of great things to come."

—

FROM *MISTY OF CHINCOTEAGUE*
(FIRST PUBLISHED 1947)

Marguerite's next book was arguably the most consequential of her long career, and it came remarkably soon after the first edition of *Justin Morgan Had a Horse* debuted. Published in 1947, *Misty of Chincoteague* was not only the book that changed Marguerite's life and made her a household name and a bestselling author, but it was also the book that changed the fortunes of an entire island community, virtually overnight and seemingly forever.

Misty also influenced and informed countless generations of horse-loving children who pilgrimaged with their parents to Chincoteague Island, Virginia, hoping (the children, that is; perhaps less so their parents) to come home with a pony just like the story's main horse character. The book still inspires great numbers of people to travel to Chincoteague, take "Misty tours" to view the wild ponies on neighboring Assateague Island, and perhaps even buy one of their own during the now famous "Pony Penning Day." Those who do not (or cannot afford to) buy a wild pony often buy a Breyer Animal Creations plastic "Misty" pony instead. (More on the Breyer model "Misty mania" in a later chapter.)

An Idea Is Born

Misty of Chincoteague had a surprisingly simple origin story. Dr. Mary Alice Jones of Rand McNally overheard a snippet about rounding up wild ponies while attending a dinner party. Jones was not only Marguerite's editor at that time and one of the most-respected book editors of the day, but also Marguerite's dear friend and confidante, and when Sid and Marguerite moved to Wayne, Jones was a regular dinner guest at their home. Indeed, one of the reasons the Henrys moved to Wayne was its proximity to Chicago and Jones. Marguerite was able to visit Jones in her office in Chicago or conduct research at the Chicago Public Library in an easy day's travel from home.

Although the Chicago Public Library was one of many libraries that Marguerite haunted over the years, it was perhaps the most important. In the essay "The Baker's Dozen" (April 26, 1968) Marguerite joked about her frequent library patronage. *"My husband says that if I ever become one of the ten most-wanted criminals the laws need only send out an alert to tell all the librarians in the world."*

Marguerite was able to travel to the Chicago Public Library from Wayne quite easily in the 1940s and 1950s, as there were regular commuter trains to and from the city that departed from the village depot not far from her house. Marguerite could have lunch in Chicago and be back in Wayne by the late afternoon. (Commuter trains stopped running on that line long ago; only freight trains run by the Wayne station today. The abandoned train tracks became part of the Illinois Prairie Path rail-to-trail system that Elizabeth Holmes, a longtime Wayne friend of Marguerite's, was instrumental in creating in the late 1960s. The Prairie Path is one of the oldest rail-trails in the nation and was even cited by President Lyndon Johnson in his 1965 message on "Conservation and Natural Beauty in Our Country." Marguerite would dedicate a later book—*Black Gold*—to Sam Holmes, husband of Elizabeth Holmes, and their son Brad.)

As one of the *Misty* origin stories goes (there are a few different versions), Jones listened in as a fellow dinner guest talked about an annual roundup of wild ponies on an island off the coast of Virginia. The ponies were herded into the water from their home on the uninhabited Assateague Island and swum across the channel to neighboring (populated) Chincoteague Island by so-called "saltwater cowboys" each July. There they were auctioned off at an event called "Pony Penning Day," with all auction proceeds benefiting the Chincoteague Volunteer Fire Department.

It sounded like a story that might interest Marguerite, thought Jones, who recounted what she'd overheard to Marguerite a few weeks later when the two met at her office in Chicago. (The recounting might also have taken place over dinner with Marguerite and Sid at their home in Wayne—sources vary as to the time and place the conversation occurred.) Whatever the actual location of that consequential first chat, Marguerite was immediately enthusiastic about writing a story based around the event, as was Sid, who urged Marguerite to visit the island and take the local Wayne horsewoman and pony expert Louise "Blondie" Coffin along. Marguerite decided to invite Dennis as well as he had moved from New York to Virginia and could potentially capture the possible story in pictures while they were on the island. Dennis was immediately game to join the expedition. (Many of his drawings in the book were from Marguerite's experiences, as well as his own. For example, Marguerite caught a seahorse and put him a glass of water by her bed at the inn where they were staying, only to awaken and find baby seahorses clinging to the curtains of her room the following morning. The incident inspired Dennis's drawing of a seahorse that appears on the last page of *Misty of Chincoteague*.)

Marguerite took endless notes about the islands as she and her travel companions spent days looking for wild ponies (*"ponies plunging"* and *"ponies streaking"* and *"a sky that leaves one a little breathless"*). She talked just as endlessly with Chincoteague residents in conversations she later described in her book *A Pictorial Life Story of Misty*, published several decades (1976) after the original *Misty* book debuted.

Marguerite booked a room at Miss Molly's Inn Bed and Breakfast on Main Street in Chincoteague for her first (and her later) exploration of the inhabited island in the story. (Today fans may rent the official "Marguerite Henry Room," a "grand room" complete with a king-size bed, lace curtains, and a private sitting area—although it is almost always booked. The "Miss Molly" was Mollie Rowley, who ran the boarding house and had quite a story of her own. Rowley was not allowed to marry while her father was alive, and when she finally did wed, her husband, Wilmer Earnest Davis, was murdered by a worker at the Reedville Fish Plant, which he managed. That was in 1938, just a few years after their marriage. Molly lived many decades more after his death—a much-loved Chincoteague resident. Bestselling novelist Lee Smith—*Fair and Tender Ladies, The Last Girls*, and most recently, *Silver Alert*—recalled the story of Miss Molly among the many Chincoteague tales she'd heard growing up from her grandmother Virginia Elizabeth "Gig" Marshall Smith, who also ran a boarding house in

Chincoteague after her own husband killed himself. Molly and Gig were especially close, according to Smith. "Miss Molly was a kind of cousin," Smith recalled. "She was very sweet to my grandmother." Smith, who now lives part-time in Virginia and part-time in North Carolina, visited Chincoteague each summer as a child and holds many fond memories of the island, its people, and especially its food. "People were huge on Chincoteague, because they ate so much," Gig wrote in a remembrance of her life on the island that included recipes for oyster pie. Although Lee Smith and Marguerite never met, Smith cites Marguerite as an inspiration for her own writing career. "I'd heard all about Marguerite, and of course I loved *Misty*, and I loved hearing about Misty," she said.)

During that first visit to the island, Marguerite spent a great deal of time trying to figure out how she could turn the story of wild ponies and a pony roundup into a story about a young boy and girl. While she was walking around town, interviewing various local townspeople, she happened upon two attractive teenagers named Maureen and Paul. It turned out that they lived with their grandfather Clarence Beebe and grandmother Ida Beebe at the Beebe Ranch on a road not far from Miss Molly's Inn.

"Grandpa Beebe," as Marguerite (or "Mag'rit," as Grandpa called her) would find, was not only the owner of a pony ranch on Chincoteague but he proved to be an invaluable source of information on the island and the history of the wild ponies (not to mention the local lingo, which Marguerite copied into notebooks meticulously). Beebe's grandchildren Paul and Maureen helped train the ponies that he later sold.

When Marguerite met Maureen and Paul, they were riding the same pony bareback, she later recalled. She told the siblings that she had come to the island to write a book about the wild ponies and Chincoteague Island, and perhaps one pony in particular—the gold-and-white foal that she'd seen and worried might be auctioned off. *"Suppose some parent with a clumsy clod of a child bought Misty in the auction tomorrow and had no idea of waiting until she grew strong enough to be ridden,"* Marguerite frets in *A Pictorial Life Story of Misty*. As she noted in *Pictorial,* Maureen and Paul seemed singularly unimpressed with her idea, and her first impression of them wasn't a particularly memorable one. Marguerite didn't even think of including the children in her book until Grandpa Beebe broached the idea in conversation.

It was Clarence Beebe and his wife Ida who helped move Marguerite's story along—they were, in fact, not only critical to the book's narrative, but to its success, especially Grandpa Beebe's idea that Paul and Maureen should feature as characters. Grandpa Beebe and Marguerite shook hands on a deal for the gold-and-white foal. *"There was no bill of sale. No bargaining. Just $150 offered and accepted,"* Marguerite wrote in *Pictorial,* and she even breezily told Grandpa Beebe that writing her book would be an easy task, especially writing Paul and Maureen into the story because, *"They will be me when I was eleven!"* (That was, of course, wishful thinking, since when Marguerite was eleven she had been sickly and housebound.)

Grandpa Beebe—*"wiry, spry-legged as a grasshopper,"* as Marguerite described him—proved to be a brilliant find, and as charming as he was knowledgeable about both ponies and life. His grandchildren were the characters Marguerite needed at the center of her book, and his words were what lit up the pages. Marguerite kept lists of Grandpa and Grandma Beebe's words and phrases that she looked to insert at various places in the narrative: *"Upon my soul!" "Good gracious me!"* and *"Facts are fine, fer as they go, but they're like water bugs skitterin' atop the water. Legends now, they go deep down and pull up the heart of the story."* Their words were not only authentic but wonderfully poetic as well.

Misty on the Mainland

Grandpa Beebe kept his word and a few months after Marguerite's visit to the island he shipped the still quite-young Misty (she was around four months old) to Marguerite in Wayne by way of a railroad box car. It was an arrangement that they had both agreed would only be temporary. Misty would live with Marguerite for as long as Marguerite needed her to finish her book (making Misty the first and most famous, but not the last, "animal-muse" that Marguerite employed while writing over the years). It was perhaps an odd deal to make, but as Grandpa Beebe noted to Marguerite, he felt the money paid for Misty would be useful to help with his grandchildren's education. And of course, it was part of the plan that Misty would eventually be returned to the Beebes, where she would be trained to be ridden and someday bred.

Although Marguerite wrote that she and Grandpa Beebe *"shook hands over $150,"* her publisher Rand McNally actually paid Grandpa Beebe for the "use" of Misty—a check for three hundred and fifty dollars, which was a handsome, though not outrageous, sum at the time, equal to around five thousand dollars today.

Several months later, when it was time for Misty to be shipped to Wayne, there was one obstacle: Marguerite didn't have a barn on her property. But her neighbors the Quayles did, and they offered its use. The Quayle children and their friends even helped to clean up the two-stall structure, especially eager to lend a hand when they heard that a wild pony from Virginia was about to arrive—a pony described by Marguerite in glowing, even fanciful, terms.

But when the "wild pony" arrived looking ragged and sad on a cold rainy day in November 1946, Marguerite had some serious misgivings. Misty had traveled four days on the train before arriving in the nearby town of Geneva, and she looked very much worse for wear. Marguerite had driven to Geneva from Wayne to help with transferring Misty to the Railway Express truck that would take her to the Quayles' barn, and she was truly shocked at the sight of the filly. When Misty stepped out of the rough crate that Grandpa Beebe had made and marked with a "C," Marguerite thought the bedraggled, rough-coated, decidedly sorry-looking foal looked nothing like the gold-and-white pony she recalled seeing just a few months earlier on the island. She could find no trace of the "map of the United States" on Misty's withers—a white marking that had captivated Marguerite—and the filly's coat looked more gray than gold. Misty was also terribly small—about the same size as Pixie, the Henrys' dog at the time. Sid remarked that Misty looked less like a pony and more like a "Siberian goat."

Marguerite felt sorry for the cold, lonely pony and a bit guilty as well. What had she done, taking the tiny foal so far from home and away from everything and everyone she'd known? And, of course, Marguerite was also wondering how she might turn such a woebe-gone creature into a good book.

The author ended up spending the night in the Quayles' stable with Misty, keeping the pony company and hoping that somehow the story she'd had in mind might still work out.

The next day dawned on a more promising note—when Misty awoke in the strange little barn, she gave Marguerite a kick when Marguerite led her out of her stall. Marguerite took this as a good omen. She related this story in *A Pictorial Life Story of Misty* (published four years after Misty's death), recalling not just Misty's inauspicious arrival in Wayne but the stir she occasioned among the neighborhood children who came around to meet the filly that first morning. *"Children appeared as if by magic. They wanted to help get her ready for her arrival. There were sisters Susie with her mop of dark curly hair and Judy with her flaxen braids; Tex, the gangling one with the deep-set eyes; Eddie and Arthur like roly-poly pups,"* Marguerite wrote, name-checking them all.

The budding young equestrians whom Marguerite named grew up to be accomplished riders as adults: Judy Martin of the "flaxen braids" became a top pony breeder and an alternate on the Olympic Equestrian Team, and the young Mary Jon "Jonnie" Quayle Edwards took up eventing and remained a serious rider all her life. Now in her eighties and living in a shore town in Connecticut, Edwards not only teaches riding but rides almost every day too. In her stable of horses there is a pinto pony—named Misty, of course. Martin and Edwards were two of the many neighborhood children who occasionally found their way astride Misty—on rides that were sanctioned and some that were not.

When Misty moved from the Quayles' barn to the stable that was eventually built behind Marguerite's house, the two friends would sneak on board the pony, riding her around and around in her stall, Edwards recalled. Afterward the girls would knock on Marguerite's door (they called her "Mrs. Henry") and officially request permission to ride Misty. "Marguerite said, 'It looks like you've already ridden Misty; you can clean my house today,'" Martin recalled. The girls didn't do much cleaning, "But absolutely what she said was right."

Edwards remembered "Mrs. Henry" as a very nice but not very grandmotherly sort of older woman. "She wasn't the kind of woman you'd want to sit in her lap," said Edwards. She was also the rare grownup who didn't have children at home, which meant she didn't have to cook for her family, said Martin, who had asked her parents why they couldn't eat lunch and dinner at the Dunham Woods Riding Club "every day like the Henrys do." She had been told it was because the Henrys had no children—not that it was (also) because Marguerite did not cook.

Finding Friday

After Misty had been in Wayne for several months and had settled in nicely, Marguerite and Sid took their annual trip south to Florida so that Sid could play golf. Although Marguerite was loathe to leave Misty, she found a local farmer she trusted with the pony's care, and their trip proved propitious. While on vacation in Florida, Marguerite found the horse she'd been waiting for all her life, and much like Misty, she found him entirely by accident.

Marguerite was writing, or trying to write, *Misty of Chincoteague* during their Florida idyll. Sid played golf while Marguerite sat at her desk, missing Misty and finding it hard to write about a pony without the real pony before her. So she went off in search of a horse or a pony to serve as an inspiration and discovered much more than that when she found Friday, a tall mannerly black Morgan horse, at Fred Tejan's nearby barn.

The trainer and horseman Fred Tejan stabled his horses at a polo grounds near where Marguerite and Sid were vacationing. Tejan was a bit of star in the equine world at the time when he and Marguerite first became acquainted. A former cattleman and bronc rider from Oklahoma, Tejan was also a good friend of Will Rogers, the entertainer and humorist. Tejan and Rogers performed together sometimes and played polo together as well. Tejan had become one of the most famous polo players in the country, and at one point, he had a string of three hundred polo ponies.

"Any good cow pony will make a polo pony," Tejan told Craig E. Taylor, who profiled Tejan in *The Baltimore Sun* (August 15, 1948) when Tejan traveled from Florida to Maryland to revive polo playing in that state. Tejan was playing competitively at the time of the interview—he played well into his late sixties. When he died of a heart attack in 1955

at seventy-five years of age, he was still working with horses at a ranch near Carmel, California. (The title of Tejan's obituary read: *"Cowboy Friend of Will Rogers Stricken, Dies."* Oddly, there was no mention of his greatness as a horse trainer or polo player.)

One of the horses in Tejan's string at the time of Marguerite's Florida visit was the handsome gelding Friday, whom Marguerite took to almost immediately. When Marguerite explained to Tejan that she needed a horse to inspire her work, Tejan offered to let her either ride or groom Friday, and Marguerite chose both. After she'd spent several weeks with the Morgan (the most blissful days of vacation she'd ever spent, Marguerite said later), it was Sid who proposed that they should buy Friday and have him shipped home to Wayne on the train. Once more, Sid seemed to know best what would make Marguerite happy. Although he didn't say much (he was a man of few words by all reports), Sid always paid close attention to Marguerite.

Friday's introduction to life in Wayne proved a bit rocky. Unlike Misty, who had traveled by truck from the Geneva station to Wayne, when Friday arrived in Geneva, he was ridden the seven or so miles to his new home by Bill Winquist, the master of Wayne's Dunham Woods Riding Club. It was a grueling journey, and Winquist announced he was less than impressed by his mount. He even told Marguerite that she'd made a terrible mistake in buying the horse. Friday was quite wild, Winquist said. Apparently, the Morgan had acted up, bucking and shying—clearly nervous with a strange rider and an unfamiliar busy road.

Marguerite forgave Friday and blamed Winquist (whom she actually greatly admired) and said she'd never had such problems with Friday herself. After all, as Tejan had told her, *"There's not a mean bone in Friday's body. He's the most honest horse who ever looked through a bridle"* (*A Pictorial Life Story of Misty*). Edward Richardson, one of the young neighborhood "Misty gang" and later Misty's regular rider, remembered Friday as a "big gentle horse," although he noted Friday did shy sometimes. "He could really jump around, but she was used to that," Richardson recalled, referring to Marguerite.

Marguerite not only soon forgave Winquist for his negative review of her new horse but also began a short story starring a veterinarian named "Dr. William Winquist" in his honor. She didn't tell him and had planned to surprise Winquist with the story, except he died before the story was finished. (Marguerite later named a character Winquist in *Brown Sunshine of Sawdust Valley,* her very last book.)

It didn't take long for Marguerite and Friday to re-establish their Florida bond, and whenever Friday was spooky or stubborn, Marguerite sang to him, and that calmed them both down. Whenever faced with walking over a bridge and Friday refusing to go forward, planting his front hooves, Marguerite would sing the same hymn, "Onward Christian Soldiers," and her black horse would cross *"as pert as you please,"* said Marguerite.

There was a great deal of such hymn singing over the years.

Misty and Friday got on immediately, with Misty proving the particularly lovestruck one of the two. Horse and pony lived in the Quayles' barn until one day, soon after the publication of *Misty of Chincoteague,* the Quayles told Marguerite that the duo had to move on, as the Quayle children were getting a horse of their own. Marguerite understood; furthermore, it seemed like the right time to build her own barn, and after all, just about everyone in Wayne had a stable on their land.

Marguerite had a spacious three-stall barn built with the proceeds from the book (aka "Misty Money") by a local man named Svenson who Marguerite noted was amused by the idea that Misty's story had paid his bill. When the little stable was finally completed, Marguerite hung the aforementioned sign that Dennis had made on Misty's door: *"Food for the Hungry/Lodging for the Weary/Good Keeping for Horses."* (The barn still stands in the same place today, a short distance behind what once was the Henry house, but it was converted into an artist's studio long ago.)

A Book with Cultural Significance

The speed with which Marguerite wrote *Misty* was impressive; it was published less than two years after her first visit to the island. But many of the books that followed took Marguerite even less time. While she often described herself as *"plodding,"* Marguerite was a remarkably fast writer—and rewriter. She wrote multiple drafts of her books before turning in a final manuscript, often with Sid and her sister Gertrude as her first readers.

Marguerite wrote about handing her first draft of *Misty* to Sid and watching him read it to find out whether or not it was good—and then the indescribable joy she felt when she saw a tear run down his cheek as he turned the pages. Sid knew better than anyone that the story of Paul and Maureen and their keen wish for a pony was, in many ways, the story of Marguerite herself.

The story of Misty was also the dream of every pony-mad child in the world. It was Marguerite's trademark fiction based on fact—or perhaps the other way around—but that scarcely seemed to matter to either the author or her readers. As Marguerite noted in the book's foreword: *"All the incidents in this story are real. They did not happen in just the order they are recorded, but they all happened at one time or another on the little island of Chincoteague."* It was a cleverly worded sort of disclaimer, though no young reader—or parent or librarian—likely thought much about it, or for that matter, took it to heart.

Marguerite chose to open *Misty* with the story of how ponies came to be on Assateague Island—by way of the shipwreck of a Spanish galleon. It was one of the generally accepted legends that Grandpa Beebe had told her when she first visited Chincoteague—except much later it turned out to be true. In 2022, a French researcher named Nicolas Delsol discovered a genetic connection between the wild ponies of the Virginia island of Assateague and Spanish ponies almost by accident, thanks to *Misty of Chincoteague*. Delsol had been reading Marguerite's book, he said in an interview in *The Washington Post* (August 6, 2022). *"It's a nice story,"* noted Delsol, adding, *"I learned quite a lot of things during my research, especially how the book had such a strong cultural significance on children's literature in the United States."*

Delsol found the DNA connection between the ponies in two very different places while researching the results of genetic tests on animal remains that had been discovered on Haiti, among them, a tooth that belonged to a Spanish horse. The remains on Haiti showed a link to the ponies on Chincoteague. *"It was amusing to find it mentioned in a novel,"* Delsol said. *"Kind of surprising when you relate it to the high-tech research we are doing."* The fact that her book—a semi-fictional narrative for children—had informed the findings of a modern-day French researcher would have doubtless pleased Marguerite quite a bit.

While Delsol's discovery helped legitimize the story of how the wild ponies came to live on Assateague Island, there is no question that today's wild ponies are of a different breed than those from long ago—and, for that matter, from the ponies that were on the island when Marguerite visited in 1946. Other horses have periodically been introduced to the island by various individuals. Ohio restaurateur Bob Evans, for example, donated over forty Mustangs in the 1970s after the herd was nearly decimated by equine infectious anemia (EIA), a blood-borne infectious viral disease. The herd has since been "refreshed" with the introduction of new ponies several more times in order to diversify the genetic pool and thereby ensure the broader health of the herd.

There are differences—both small and large—between the story that Marguerite wrote and the real people and places that are named in the book's pages. For example, Maureen and Paul of Marguerite's story lived with and worked with their grandfather, helping to train ponies, just as the real-life Maureen and Paul had, but while the fictional Maureen and Paul were determined to buy a pony of their own, that was *not* the case with the real brother and sister. Other facts were "adjusted" as well. In the book, Misty was sold on Pony Penning Day to someone else—until she was *not*, when it turned out her buyer won a different pony in a raffle, thereby allowing Paul and Maureen to take Misty home. This isn't quite true. Although there *is* a pony raffle held during Pony Penning each year, it had nothing to do with Misty, and of course, the real Misty did not live happily ever after with Maureen and Paul but was shipped to Marguerite in Wayne, Illinois, instead. And although she wasn't meant to stay with Marguerite for very long—just until the book was finished—she remained in Wayne for over ten years.

Riding a Legend

The reasons for Misty's extended stay were a mixture of the personal and the professional. Marguerite had grown much attached to Misty, but after the publication of the book, with interest in Misty at its peak, Marguerite also realized that the pony was a great marketing device for the book. As her former Wayne neighbor Art Richardson, brother of Ed Richardson, said admiringly, "Marguerite was a real marketing machine."

Art Richardson is a lifelong Wayne resident. His parents would travel to Wayne from Chicago at the time when there were still electric commuter trains running to Wayne. "They would take golf clubs on the train, play three rounds, and get back on the train to Chicago," he recalled. The Richardsons eventually moved to Wayne in 1939 and Richardson Senior reversed his golf commute, riding the train to and from Chicago for work.

When Misty turned three and was old enough to ride, the Richardson boys, both avid horsemen, were successively recruited to get on her, along with their friend Sid "Tex" Drexler. Art Richardson recalled that Misty grew up to be a large pony—she was around 14 hands (a "hand" is horseman's speak for four inches) when he was asked by a friend of Marguerite's to be Misty's first rider. He didn't ride her for very long as he grew too tall; his brother Ed soon took over the (unpaid) job.

At seven years of age, Art Richardson already had a reputation as a good rider. He went on to become Master of the Hunt at the Wayne Hunt Club and hunted all over the world. Richardson now keeps horses at his family's property about a mile from Marguerite's former home. He recalled Misty as a less-than-placid pony—in fact, she could be rather bad-tempered and inclined to buck. "It was a good day when I didn't get bucked off," Richardson said. Ed Richardson, who lives close to Wayne and runs the family business Richardson Electronics, had his own issues with Misty. "She would bite if you cinched the girth too tight," he recalled.

Everyone in Wayne had a horse in those days, according to Ed Richardson. "When school was out, we all went riding." Richardson, Drexler, and Marguerite would ride together three times a week, Richardson said. "She treated us like adults; she didn't talk to you like you were a child." Indeed, as Marguerite wrote in the essay "Horse Sense is Stable Thinking," published in the Wayne-DuPage Hunt newsletter, she often ran story ideas by the two boys. *"These rides provided the ideal time for a powwow whenever my story characters or the story line were causing problems,"* Marguerite wrote, adding that she might ask the boys their opinion on a particular point, such as her questions related to an early draft of *Brighty of the Grand Canyon* (which was published a few years following *Misty*): Did they think it would be all right for a mountain lion to attack Brighty while he was sleeping? The boys wanted to know who would win. Marguerite's reply was surprisingly graphic: *"There'd be a snarling, howling savage fight... claws ripping, hooves flailing, blood spurting..."* she replied. In the end, Brighty would roll on the lion in a nearby pond and drown him, Marguerite concluded. The boys seemed shocked. Did they want her to forgo such a scene? They absolutely did not—in fact, the group even play-acted the fight on the lawn in front of Marguerite's house.

Misty Parties

Ed Richardson not only rode Misty but participated in the many Misty birthday and holiday parties that Marguerite held in her front yard (Mole Meadow). The birthday parties began in the wake of the publication of the book and continued for years. Dozens and dozens of children showed up at Marguerite's house, parents in tow. "They closed the school every year on Misty's birthday," Richardson recalled. The children came to eat cake, watch Misty perform the tricks that Sid had taught her (standing on a stool, "shaking hands"), and their parents bought Marguerite's books. These gatherings were often as not covered by the local press.

Marguerite arranged to have Misty give each child in attendance a "hoofagraph" (aka Misty's hoofprint) on a card, and in some cases they got one of the so-called "Denny" cards—cards made by Wesley Dennis that depicted Misty's face (as well as other horses). Sometimes Marguerite took "The Misty Show" on the road to fairs and department stores, and she would occasionally commission both Richardson boys to dress up as Paul and Maureen Beebe and act out parts of the story. Art Richardson noted that he played Maureen until he got too tall; then the role fell to his brother. "Marguerite decided if she wanted to sell books, she had to put on an event," Richardson recalled.

Art Richardson specifically remembers one trip he took with Misty and Marguerite to Marshall Fields, the famed upscale department store in downtown Chicago (long since closed). "I don't know how we got Misty in the elevator, but we did," said Richardson. The store had a book department where he and Misty and Marguerite delivered hoofagraphs and sold books. It was always about selling books—and it worked. *Misty of Chincoteague* became a perennial hit; there were twenty-five printings of the book between 1947 and 1973, and although Misty died in 1972, that same year she became one of the bestselling Breyer model horses of all time.

Columnist Lucy Key Miller (*Chicago Tribune,* July 17, 1952) covered one of the many Misty parties held at Mole Meadow. Marguerite was celebrating Misty's birthday inside the living room of her "farmhouse" in Wayne, reported Miller in a column entitled "Carrots for Candles," and noted the event in rather breathless prose: *"Each year, wearing a paper hat and surrounded by enchanted children, the once wild and timid little horse from the faraway island of Chincoteague comes serenely indoors to nibble on her birthday cake with carrot candles,"* she wrote. Misty was due to be escorted to the Wayne carnival by local horseman Eddie Pacinas, who would allow children to take a turn at riding Misty—or least sitting on her, Miller noted. (The name Eddie Pacinas is a familiar one in Marguerite's former circles;

The Echo

Literature

Man to Super-man
(Apologies to Joyce Kilmer.)

I think that I have never yet,
A mate for Charley Hawtre met,
A girl who would, through lack of fear,
Assume the role and call him dear;
A one, who in her heart could feel
Him worth the cooking of a meal;
Who in her mind, her heart, her soul,
Proclaim him king, and play her role.
Poems are made by fools like me;
But only God could make Hawtrey!

JACK WILCOX.

Femininity

I mark the brilliant color of her cheek,
The pretty, tilted smub of powdered nose,
The childish treble voice, so soft and meek,
The silken swish of super-stylish clothes.
I note the bright cascade of bobbing locks,
The charming smile of ultra-carmine lips,
The naughty lure of dainty rolled socks.
The cutex manicure of finger tips.
I see the arch of brow so thin and black,
The lashes darkened, long, and curling sweet;
I see the wrap of fur — from throat turned back—
The arctics flapping, clicking down the street.

But 'neath it all a heart of gold has she,
And Lord, how I love her — and she loves me!

MARGUERITE BREITHAUPT.

Page 172

The Echo

ARTHUR HERMAN NICOLAUS Miller High
"Artie" Course of True Love
Pres. Junior Class '22; Senior Class
Play '22; Junior Prom Committee '22; Senior Class Play '22. What the heck is he,
anyhow? (Ah, fair reader, unto many is it
given to ax that question, but unto few indeed is the answer revealed.)

"The world is a looking-glass"
Gosh! what a life ahead of him!

REGINALD ARTHUR TOFTE
Barbenroth H. S.
"Reggie" Dessert Course
Carnegie medal for life-saving of Echo;
Crown Prince, Philosophers' Club.

"Nowher so wys a man as he ther n'as
And yet he seemed wyser than he was."

MARGUERITE AGATHA BREITHAUPT
"Bryt-top"
Graduate: School of Scandal
Class Profit '22; Damon, Pythias & Co.;
Syncopatia Literary Society.

"If to her there 'ome female errors fall,
Look on her face, and you'll forget them
all."

LESLIE LeROY LAURENT JEROME SAXE RIESELBACH
"Leelee" Squair Corner High School
Teachers' Pet 1921; Coach Junior Girls'
Basketball Team; Scarlet Club.

"His eyes as stars of twilight fair,
Like twilight, too, his dusty hair."

Page 166

The Echo

LOUISE C. BOERS..............Kindergarten
"Poots" South Division
Kindergarten Association; Goodfellowship
League.

ALMA BORNITZKE..............Deaf
"Al" Pewaukee
Philacophia; Y. W. C. A.; Secretary Philacophia.

GLADYS M. BOWMAN..............Primary
"Glad" Albany
Erodelphia; Goodfellowship League; Y. W. C. A.

MARGUERITE BREITHAUPT......Journalism
"Marge" Riverside
Pythia; Le Cercle Francais; English Club;
Dramatic Club; President Pythia; Vice-President
Dramatic Club; Dramatic Club Play; Union Vodvil;
Senior Class Play; French Play.

/ 1–3 /
The Echo Annual
yearbook shows
Marguerite Breithaupt
(aka "Marge") was a busy
and popular student at
Milwaukee (Wisconsin)
State Normal School (now
University of Wisconsin-
Milwaukee), writing and
acting in plays, penning
poems, and reporting
for the school paper. The
depictions of her show
she also had the requisite
poofy-bang haircut that
was popular in the day.
◆ *Courtesy of the Wisconsin*
Historical Society

/ 4 /
Marguerite and Sidney (Sid) Crocker Henry, not long after they first met at "fishing camp" in the early 1920s.

4

5

THE MILWAUKEE JOURNAL

Left to Right—Mrs. Raymond L. Mass, Wahlaw, whose husband has been making attractive pastel portraits of well known folk. (Guttenstein portrait.) Miss Marguerite Breithaupt, daughter of Mr. and Mrs. Louis Breithaupt, Downer-av, whose marriage to Sidney ...cker Henry will take place May 5. (Klein portrait.) Miss Delores ...othy Monsen, daughter of Mr. and Mrs. O. W. Monsen, whose ...riage to Hale Kilmer will take place May 5 at the Hotel Astor. ...ein portrait.)

TWO MAY BRIDES

6

Mrs. Hale B. Kilmer.   (Stein photo.)

Mrs. Sidney C. Henry.   (Stein photo.)

M RS. HALE B. KILMER before her marriage on Wednesday was Miss Dolores Monsen, daughter of Mr. and Mrs. O. W. Monsen. The ceremony was performed by the Rev. Charles Beals at the Astor hotel. The couple will reside at the Breakers, Rogers Park, Chicago. Miss Marguerite Breithaupt, daughter of Mr. and Mrs. Louis Breithaupt, was married on Saturday to Sidney Crocker Henry.

/ 5 & 6 /
The announcement of Marguerite's engagement in *The Milwaukee Journal* in April 1923 (top—she is in the middle) and of her wedding (she is the bride on the right) in an unknown Wisconsin paper in May 1923.

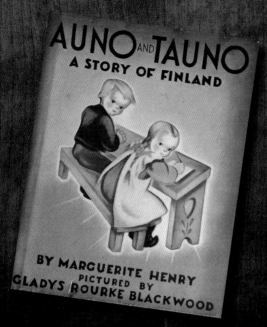

/ 7 /
The original edition cover
for *Auno and Tauno*
(Albert Whitman, 1940).

/ 8 /
A family photograph taken at Sid Henry's mother
Ida's funeral in 1939. From left to right:
Elmer Henry, Sid and Marguerite Henry,
and Margaret and Roy Henry.
♦ *Courtesy of Ann Keckonen*

The original edition cover
for *Geraldine Belinda*
(Platt & Munk Co, Inc, 1942).

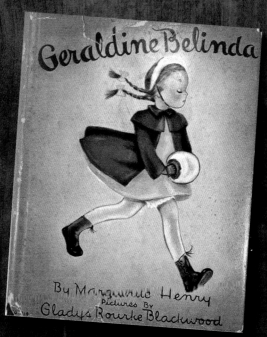

The original edition cover
for *Birds at Home*
(M.A. Donohue & Co., 1942).

Although most of Marguerite's books featured horses, she wrote a few books about other creatures, including an early one about the habits and behavior of twenty-one common North American birds. *Birds at Home* featured color illustrations by Jacob Bates Abbott (known for his work in field guides for bird identification).

/ 12 /
The original edition cover
for *The Little Fellow*
(John C. Winston Co., 1945).

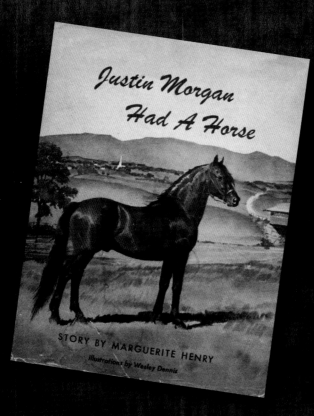

/ 13 /
The original edition cover
for *Justin Morgan Had a Horse*
(Wilcox & Follet Co., 1945).

Marguerite was always game to read her books
to anyone who asked—and she was
always impeccably dressed.

/ 15 & 16 /

In middle age (and much later) Marguerite retained
a youthful appearance and was often assumed to be much
younger than her chronological age. She was always stylishly
attired and her hair (which was variously brown or blonde over
the years) was always perfectly coiffed, which a press photo
from 1946 (*top*) and one from the fifties (*bottom*) demonstrate.

◆ *Bottom photo © Wolfmann Studio*

The Beebe children, who inspired the main characters in what would become Marguerite's bestselling book *Misty of Chincoteague*, were accomplished and confident young riders—more often than not riding ponies bareback. Here Paul and Maureen are with Black Comet.

◆ *Photo originally appeared in DEAR READERS AND RIDERS (Rand McNally, 1969)*

20

21

Misty, the real-life pony who would help inspire the bestselling book *Misty of Chincoteague*, could barely see out of the wooden enclosure that served as her stall while she traveled north by rail from Virginia to Marguerite's Illinois home. Marguerite and her husband Sid drove to meet the train the night Misty arrived, and the filly—then just a few months old—was transferred to a truck and driven home to Wayne. Sid and Marguerite's neighbors, the Quayles, were kind enough to allow Misty to live in their empty barn for a while, and their children helped make the frightened foal comfortable. Marguerite slept next to Misty that first night to make sure she was all right.

◆ *Photos © JD Pennewell (top left) and Wolfmann Studio originally appeared in* A Pictorial Life Story of Misty *(Rand McNally, 1976)*

/ 22 /
The original edition cover
for *Misty of Chincoteague*
(Rand McNally, 1947).

/ 23 /
Although as the author's "muse," Misty was only meant
to stay with Marguerite until the book about her was finished
and then return to Chincoteague, Marguerite grew very attached
to her, and the pony remained in Wayne for over ten years.

◆ *Photo originally appeared in* A PICTORIAL LIFE STORY OF MISTY
(Rand McNally, 1976)

/ 24 /

One of the rare photos of Marguerite aboard Misty
at home in Wayne. Misty was just two years old;
the perennially youthful Marguerite was 46.

◆ *Photo courtesy of the Marguerite Henry Collection,*
The Kerlan, University of Minnesota Archives

/ 25 /

The original edition cover
for *Benjamin West*
and His Cat Grimalkin
(Bobbs-Merrill, 1947).

/ 26 /
The original edition cover
for *King of the Wind*
(Rand McNally, 1948).

/ 27 /
Marguerite and Wesley Dennis made
innumerable personal appearances
at leading department stores like
Marshall Fields in Chicago. They'd not
only autograph books but often
act out scenes from the books too.

Marguerite Henry, Wesley Dennis, and Mary Alice
Jones, the longtime children's book editor at Rand
McNally, in New York when it was announced
that *King of the Wind* was being awarded the 1949
Newbery Medal. Jones was not only the editor
of many of the books Marguerite and Dennis
produced but a dear friend who also happened
to share Marguerite's love of a good hat.

♦ *Photo © Charles Meyer*

29

/ 29 /
When Marguerite was awarded the prestigious Newbery Medal
in 1949, Misty made a guest appearance alongside the author at
the American Library Association (ALA) Convention in Grand
Rapids, Michigan—to the delight of many (and the dismay of some).

◆ *Photo © Dale Rooks originally appeared in A PICTORIAL LIFE STORY OF MISTY*
(Rand McNally, 1976)

he was the highly respected horseman to whom she would later give her horse Friday.)

Misty and Marguerite were often honored guests, not only at local fairs, but at horse shows as well. A story in *The Chicago Tribune* noted that at the local Dunham Woods Horse Show in Wayne in the summer of 1954, Marguerite "and her pet" pony appeared, both dressed to the hilt. *"Mrs. Henry was the picture of chic in a gray flannel skirt and blouse, a vest of yellow suede and a visored cap of denim,"* while Misty came wearing *"rosebuds fashioned to her mane"* when they presented a youthful Betsy Hamill with a cup for her placement as Best Young Rider.

Of Misty's many public appearances, perhaps her most memorable one took place at the Grand Rapids, Michigan, American Library Association (ALA) Convention in 1949. It was the year that *King of the Wind* won the Newbery Medal, and Misty had been invited to accompany Marguerite to the convention to mark the occasion—or had she? There was some heated discussion and outright dissent as to whether the pony was a welcome guest or a part of an unwelcome publicity stunt. A photograph taken the day of Misty's guest appearance is at once comical and surreal: Misty is shown standing among a crowd of well-coiffed, mostly stiff, and mostly unsmiling women in business suits.

Whether Misty had truly been invited or not, her appearance made Art Richardson's point: Marguerite knew how to make the most of a moment, and in the case of Virginia Chase, an ALA member and prior chair of the Newbery Caldecott Medal Awards, Marguerite also knew how to get a rise out of some stuffy people as well.

Chase unleashed her fury over Misty's appearance in an indignant letter to Helen Chase (no relation) of *The Booklist*, an ALA publication: *"In case you wondered if CLA has lost its wits by having Misty there, you will be interested to know that the CLA Board to the last man decidedly voted against the horse and was assured by Headquarters that she would not appear. This first I knew she was coming was when I read in Mr. Cory's memo in the October Bulletin...I hope no one else at Headquarters thinks we wanted the horse or even lifted a finger to get her there."*

Helen Chase gently replied to Virginia Chase that Misty had, in fact, been a great hit, enjoyed by everyone—save, perhaps, their publishing rival, MacMillan Books, as *Misty of Chincoteague* was not only a bestseller but after less than ten years in print, nearly a million copies had been sold.

The In-Between Book:
Benjamin West and His Cat Grimalkin

In between their two major collaborations, *Misty of Chincoteague* and *King of the Wind*, Marguerite and Wesley Dennis collaborated on a much shorter but still-charming book called *Benjamin West and His Cat Grimalkin*. Based on the true story of the American painter Benjamin West, who grew up in a Quaker household in Pennsylvania and went on to become the President of the Royal Academy of England, the painter to King George III, and the "Father of American painting," it was one of just a few of Marguerite's books that did not feature a horse. It did, however, star a rather useful cat.

Marguerite was inspired to tell the story of Benjamin West after she read that he'd been taught by Native Americans how to paint and had to make his own brushes because his parents would not buy him art supplies, as his wish to become an artist was a violation of their Quaker beliefs. And it also happened that Benjamin West had a cat whose tail was long and voluminous—and, she imagined, could be put to good use as a paint brush.

The cat's tail was the necessary hook for Marguerite. She'd actually discovered the story while researching another biography that she'd been commissioned to write: *Robert Fulton: Boy Craftsman*, published in 1945 by Bobbs-Merrill (which was later purchased by MacMillan Publishing). This wasn't the least bit uncommon; Marguerite often found additional ideas while researching a book and had bulging file folders of story possibilities. Some were just notes; some were ideas much more fully fleshed-out. She was always racing ahead to find the next story—even when she was in the middle of writing another.

The Benjamin West book required a fair amount of revising. According to a memorandum regarding "Grimalkin," dated January 20, 1946, from associate editor Rosemary York: *"It seems plain to me that Marguerite Henry's manuscript bears criticizing. She has perhaps unconsciously fallen into the formula of the Childhood series and so the stories become centered around Benjamin West instead of the cat. Neither of us thinks West is exciting enough to belong in the series..."* York wrote.

It's an interesting criticism since Marguerite was always very focused on the animal characters in her stories. Was it that she didn't feel as much for cats as she did horses and dogs? (Marguerite did at one point have a cat she called "Mom Cat" who appears in a few photographs.) Marguerite revised *Benjamin West* several more times, and in February 1946, Marguerite wrote to her publisher that she still had "a great deal of work to do on the manuscript," and furthermore noted that artists who were able to draw cats well were particularly difficult to find. Marguerite was working solo at the time, without the support of an artist, and perhaps that was another reason why the book was more of a struggle for her than others.

Bobbs-Merrill had contacted Diana Thorne, but she was not available, so an executive from the publisher inquired in a memo dated July 31, 1946, *"Would Wesley Dennis do the pictures for $400?"* Dennis instead accepted compensation in the form of a split royalty with Marguerite. And so, although he was not yet as famous as Thorne in those days, Dennis got the job. (That same executive noted in another memo: *"Rosemary [York] says Marguerite told her Wesley got $2500 for Justin Morgan"*—that it was definitely not a split-royalty book like Diana Thorne's.)

Benjamin West was critically well-received—it is listed in the Library of Congress as one of the best juvenile books of 1947—but although the story has been republished in a variety of formats, it has never achieved the lasting fame of Marguerite's other books. Was it the lack of a horse or the lack of great suffering on the part of the protagonists or a lack of deep emotion in the story itself? Or was York right? Perhaps the cat wasn't sufficiently central to the story.

letters

811 N. Main
Goshen, IN 46526
September 20, 1977

Miss Marguerite Henry
c/o Rand McNally & Company
P.O. Box 7600
Chicago, Ill 60680

Dear Miss Henry:

    I am a sixth grade teacher in Goshen, Indiana, and a great admirer of your books. I have read and studied <u>King of the Wind</u> with my classes several times over the past few years.

    As a school activity I am interested in organizing a <u>Marguerite Henry Day</u> at Waterford Elementary School. I would like to know if you make personal visits to schools and if you would consider visiting us at Waterford? I have no specific dates in mind as I would like the selection to be yours if such a visit is possible.

    I appreciate your consideration of this request and will be anticipating your reply.

                    Sincerely,

                    Leonard Harms

5

KING OF THE WIND

CHAPTER FIVE

5

"Whenever the horseboys raced their horses beyond the city gates,
Sham outran them all. He outran the colts his own age
and the seasoned running horses as well.
He seemed not to know that he was an earthly creature
with four legs, like the other horses."

—

FROM *King of the Wind*
(First Published 1948)

While Marguerite was finishing the book about Benjamin West and managing Misty's many public appearances, she was also deep into the research of her next and possibly most-acclaimed work: *King of the Wind.*

The book stars a boy and a cat also named Grimalkin (as with the cat of Benjamin West), along with one of the most famous horses in history: Sham aka the Godolphin Arabian—a real-life legendary stallion who became one of the founding sires of the Thoroughbred breed.

Although the Godolphin Arabian lived in the eighteenth century, Marguerite chose to open the book in the more recent past—specifically in 1920 in Windsor, Ontario, when the two great racehorses Man o' War and Sir Barton were about to face one another. It was billed as an historic race, but Man o' War, arguably the greatest racehorse of the twentieth century, easily won. In Marguerite's telling, his owner, Samuel Riddle, was urged to race Man o' War just one more time, this time in Newmarket, England. Riddle, to whom Marguerite dedicated *King of the Wind*, declined the suggestion; Man o' War did not need an additional race to prove his worth. Marguerite imagined Riddle musing post-race about Man o' War's ancestor, the Godolphin Arabian: *"He had not raced at Newmarket either. And he had no pedigree either. It had been lost. He had to write a new one with his own blood, the blood that flowed in the veins of his sons and daughters... But it was not easy for Riddle to convince his friends that this plan was the right one. Often, he had to go back two hundred years and tell them the story of the Godolphin Arabian."*

Although the race between Man o' War and Sir Barton took place decades before *King of the Wind* was published, it was a deft way to place a long-ago story in a contemporary context. As Marguerite said in a tribute to Riddle and Man o' War in her Newbery acceptance speech: *"It was his beloved Big Red that helped to fasten draw-chains on the past. If I could make children understand that this hero of theirs was a direct descendent of the Godolphin Arabian, history would no longer sleep with closed, waxed eyelids, it would quicken to life."*

Marguerite and Riddle met while she was writing an early draft of *King of the Wind*. Marguerite had sent Riddle the opening chapter and Riddle had sent her a sternly worded reply. Marguerite's draft had suggested that Man o' War had suffered an injury and that was why he had been retired. The inference made the eighty-seven-year-old Riddle near-apoplectic. He wrote Marguerite that the idea came from someone who was *"a word of four letters beginning with 'L.'"*

The truth, Riddle said, was that Man o' War had been retired at three because of the great weight he would have been forced to carry in his next race—more than any four-year-old racehorse in history—if he were to race again. (By his fourth race he was carrying one hundred and thirty pounds—an enormous weight for a very young horse. Weight "handicapping" assumes the weight a horse carries affects the speed at which he will be able to travel; therefore, a better horse carries a heavier weight than horses with less perceived ability.) Riddle did not want to risk Man o' War breaking down. It wasn't out of fear that he kept the big horse from racing; it was because he loved the horse so much.

But Riddle softened his angry reply by issuing an invitation to Marguerite to visit him at his farm in Hialeah, Florida, if she really wanted to learn the "true" story of Man o' War, whom the world knew by the nickname "Big Red." Marguerite accepted his invitation with alacrity. But before they met, she rewrote the offending chapter and brought the revision to Riddle at his home, where she read it to him aloud. She told this story in her Newbery acceptance speech: *When I finished reading to him about his immortal Man o' War, I looked up to find a tear spilling down his cheek. Then I cried too and we were friends.*

Set Afire by a Story Idea

Although *King of the Wind* was published after *Misty of Chincoteague*, Marguerite had been thinking about the Godolphin Arabian for quite some time—long before she wrote *Misty*. It was, however, on her first trip to Chincoteague with Dennis that they first discussed the idea. Dennis told Marguerite that he'd been thinking about the Godolphin Arabian ever since he'd been approached by Walter Chrysler, the auto magnate, some years earlier to draw a portrait of the horse as a letterhead for his stud farm stationery. Chrysler was not only the founder of the eponymous automotive company but also an avid horseman and Thoroughbred breeder. His farm, North Wales Stud, was in Warrenton, Virginia, not far from the Dennis family farm. When Dennis asked his assistant to research a portrait of the Godolphin Arabian for a reference for the painting Chrysler had commissioned, the assistant uncovered the sad story of the foundation sire's life.

Before the Earl of Godolphin of Cambridgeshire, England, recognized his greatness as a sire, Sham (the original name of the Godolphin Arabian) had been subjected to years of abuse and neglect by various prior owners, including some years spent as a cart horse in Paris. It was a story that Dennis was convinced he and Marguerite could bring to life in a book. In fact, soon after he described the great horse's sad history to her, Marguerite too became obsessed with the idea of telling the story, although it took time to transform the idea into reality.

Marguerite described their mutual state of obsession in *The Illustrated Marguerite Henry*—as the artist and writer worked on *Misty*, the story of the Godolphin Arabian remained ever-present in their minds, until they could finally convince Rand McNally of its worth. *"The ups and downs of the Godolphin set Wesley and me afire,"* she wrote. *"By a happy twist of fate, we had fallen heir to a drama that clearly demanded his pictures and my words. We tackled the book with a kind of hunger."* That hunger in her partnership with Dennis was a deeper, wilder version of the bond she had formed, if only for a few years, with Rourke-Blackwood in Freeport.

Hunger seemed like an accurate word to describe the ferocity with which Marguerite tackled the research of the book. She was eager to bring to life the Cinderella-like story of a poor immigrant boy and downtrodden horse who turned out to be one of the most consequential stallions in equine history. Despite this seemingly perfect combination, Marguerite faced strong resistance from her publisher, as well as family and friends. They collectively reasoned that Marguerite's last few books—*Justin Morgan* and *Misty* and *Benjamin West*—had been successful, well-received all-American tales, and it made sense for Marguerite to stick to the same formula. She had a huge audience of avid readers for such books—why did she and Dennis care so much about a horse born so long ago, and so far away? Who among her young readers cared about Morocco, or for that matter, could even find it on a map?

The questions continued, but they failed to raise doubts in Marguerite's mind. She knew it would be a challenge to tell the story from the perspective of a boy who couldn't talk (the Godolphin Arabian's caretaker was mute). How would that work? What kind of gestures would he make? She needed to research that, as well as everything else. The research would be enormous, and enormously time-consuming, and even if Marguerite could pull it (all) off, would the book even sell?

The skepticism that Marguerite faced was that of any bestselling author who deviates from a tried-and-true formula. But the resistance she encountered made Marguerite that much more determined to write the book. For her, the prospect of undertaking prodigious research was hugely appealing—the idea of spending weeks and months in libraries looking up facts about long dead men and horses, delving deep into the history of a long-ago era and faraway places, and corresponding with academics and horsemen was, to her, a prospect nothing short of idyllic.

Marguerite read dozens of books about the period in which her characters lived and sought to understand them not simply as characters, but as people (and horses) who had *actually lived*. What made them happy? How did they feel? What did their world look like and smell like? She wanted to feel and to taste and to see things as they had.

"I read every day and every night until these ghostly people assumed substance and began to take me into their confidence," Marguerite wrote in 1969's collection of letters to fans, *Dear Readers and Riders*. She had to find a way into her characters' thoughts—and their hearts. *"I began to see the Earl of Godolphin as not just an aristocrat who owned a stable of pleasure horses. His passion was horses, blooded horses,"* Marguerite wrote.

Marguerite reached out to scholars and librarians and historians and horsemen and theologians. From one Quaker authority, Marguerite learned the plural of Quaker terms. She was schooled by a professor of comparative religion about the Koran, including references within it to the "garden" where all happy people dwell. Although there is a long list of "books consulted" and authorities thanked on the last page of *King of the Wind*, Marguerite noted it was merely a partial source list.

Marguerite didn't just read about the places and people who were to appear in her book, she sought a visual connection with them as well, covering the walls of her study with pictures of thatched houses and kitchens, and even a beauty salon where the wigs of French nobility were stored. She hung images of Arabian horses and stable boys and French aristocrats and the Earl of Godolphin "magnificent in his cascade of ruffles" as well. She scribbled notes on folders and pieces of paper from Sid's work and even on motel stationery. *King of the Wind* was a story that Marguerite knew had to be deeply felt by the reader, and so as she worked, she wanted to live the story as well. Marguerite became the characters she was describing in the book: *"At a glance I was the boy Agba feeding camel's milk to a sick foal. In quick succession I was Sham racing a gazelle across the desert..."* she shared in *Dear Readers and Riders*. Marguerite acted out Agba's work and his heartbreak as she was going about her barn chores. As she described in "The Story Behind the Godolphin Story," in her newsletter (*No. 2*):

"Even at noon when I set aside my work and went out to water my own horse, I was still in the past. It was not his eyelashes that brushed my hand as I held the water bucket but those of Sham, the fleet one. And so the anguish of writing was washed away because my story characters completely took over my life and the here-and-now grew dim."

Ahead of Its Time

King of the Wind was far more daring than Marguerite's previous books, and perhaps any of the books that followed, not only because the story took place hundreds of years earlier in faraway places that few people traveled to or even knew much about in the 1940s, but because Marguerite tried to place herself in the shoes of a poor Arab boy who was as harshly treated as his horse. It was an act of remarkable cultural sensitivity to have been achieved by a middle-class middle-aged white woman, living in a small conservative town in the Midwest in the mid-twentieth century.

Marguerite wrote a complex story of dark moments and a great deal of suffering before hope was finally restored. Even when Sham was ultimately triumphant—his worth recognized by all—Agba was still just "a varmint-in-a-hood," as the innkeeper's wife called him, mocked and abused at every turn. The illustrations by Dennis perfectly matched Marguerite's prose—by turns joyous and heartbreaking.

The hurt and heartache seems almost unbearable, and that deeply expressed sorrow in both words and images was thanks in part to Marguerite's editor, Mary Alice Jones, who insisted that the full extent of the suffering of both horse and boy should be fully depicted in art and words. Marguerite and Dennis's earliest efforts were a bit too sanitized, said Jones. For example, in Dennis's first drawing of Agba, imprisoned in the Newgate Jail, the picture didn't seem sufficiently harsh. *"Too pleasant. Looks like a library instead of a jail,"* Jones wrote in a note to Marguerite.

Jones also urged Marguerite to consider her transitions from one setting in the book to the next. As Marguerite recounted in her Newbery acceptance speech, this was the sort of detail where her editor's help proved invaluable. Marguerite shared an example of a passage when Sham boarded the ship in Tangier with other horses on his way to France. His coat was sleek and gleaming at the beginning of his journey, but then he arrived in France as a mere bag of bones. *"What happened to make them thin?"* Jones wanted to know.

Marguerite was so caught up in the story, rapidly moving from one scene to the next, that she often forgot to connect the scenes in her books—something she confessed to more than once. And she could be a bit prudish as well. For example, it was Jones who encouraged Marguerite to describe the "romance" between Sham and the mare Lady Roxana, as well as his war with the stallion Hobgoblin who was competing for her affections. Marguerite, having initially skirted both scenes, wrote them into the manuscript thanks to the urging of Jones.

The final scene of the book, which features Dennis's brilliant illustration of the Godolphin Arabian being presented to the Queen with Agba astride the great horse, was also a subject of some discussion—this time between Dennis and Marguerite. The scene wasn't something that had actually happened, but for Marguerite, even if the presentation hadn't taken place in history, she wanted to get the details right: the color of the Queen's dress, the livery worn by the groom, the color of the grass—it all necessitated a visit by Marguerite to the Chicago Public Library for confirmation.

"Of course, the Queen would be gowned and plumed in purple," Marguerite wrote in *The Illustrated Marguerite Henry,* as she was the Queen, after all. And since her meticulous research revealed that the

Earl of Godolphin's stable colors were scarlet and blue, the Dennis illustration shows the footman attired in these hues as he holds Sham's bridle for the Queen to affix a purple plume to his browband.

Across the page from this beautiful piece of art, Marguerite expressed Agba's triumphant unspoken thought: *"My name is Agba. Ba means father. I will be a father to you, Sham, and when I am grown, I will ride you before the multitudes. And they will bow before you and you will be King of the Wind!"*

Although *King of the Wind* won the most prestigious award in children's book publishing and was a bestselling book reprinted multiple times, neither the movie it inspired (1990) nor the two Breyer models—Sham and Roxana, the mare to whom the Godolphin Arabian was bred—came close to the success of those of *Misty of Chincoteague*. Was the story too exotic? Was it too hard for a child to relate to so much suffering and the pain? In many ways, *King of the Wind* was a book ahead of its time.

The Newbery

The critical response to *King of the Wind* was uniformly positive. *"A book to delight all horse lovers,"* stated the *Lansing State Journal* (December 19, 1948), and *"Unequalled for glamour and romanticism,"* wrote Dorothy Jones for *The Jackson Sun* (Sept 4, 1949), and *The Bakersfield Californian* (March 11, 1949) noted, *"Fact, legend and fiction are artfully combined in this fast-moving tale which is above average among the many horse stories published every year."* Marguerite's readers chimed in as well. According to *The Hackensack (NJ) Record*, *King of the Wind* was the best-liked book by Hillsdale, New Jersey, fifth graders in the librarian's poll. And, as mentioned, it won the much-coveted Newbery Medal, the highest honor bestowed upon a children's book author—an award that, at the time, had never been won by an author from the Midwest, and in fact, never one from outside the East Coast. It was this award that would also link Marguerite's two bestselling books to date: When the Medal award ceremony took place at the Pantlind Hotel in Grand Rapids, Michigan (where Misty was stabled in a room on the hotel's first floor), Rand McNally made the formal transfer of Misty's ownership from the publisher (that had fronted the money for Misty) to Marguerite.

"*It was the least we could do for our number-one author!*" Joe Landes, then-publisher of Rand McNally's trade book department, wrote. "*The ownership of Misty belonged to the woman who loved the pony with all her heart.*"

Sea Star: Orphan of Chincoteague

Marguerite had vowed that she would not write a *Misty* sequel, or so she said in her introduction to *Sea Star: Orphan of Chincoteague*: "Misty, *I thought, was complete in itself. Let the boys and girls dream their own wonderful sequels.*" But a sort-of-*Misty* sequel presented itself when Marguerite learned of an orphan foal that had been found next to his dead mother at Tom's Cove on Chincoteague Island. It was a story that she decided—or perhaps her publisher decided—needed to be told. It was also an opportunity to reprise all the familiar characters, in the same beloved place, much as if no time had passed.

In the opening scene of *Sea Star*, which was published the year after *King of the Wind* (1949), Paul and Maureen Beebe are braiding Misty's tail—never mind that at the time of writing the real Misty was still living in Wayne with Marguerite and Maureen and Paul were much older than depicted. *Sea Star* was a book to recapture the magic of the character of Misty (who actually and perhaps unsurprisingly gets a great deal more ink than the orphan Sea Star). The book's main action focuses on Paul and Maureen and what happens when two men, Mr. Van Meter and Mr. Jacobs, come to Chincoteague to propose featuring Misty in a movie—although Paul and Maureen later discover the men also want to buy Misty and take her to New York.

"We'd want to take her to schools and libraries where boys and girls could meet her. We'd want to fix a stall for her in theaters where her picture was showing so boys and girls could see the real Misty. It might be a long time before she could come back," the men say to Paul and Maureen in the book. Thus the fictional Misty is loaded into a New York-bound crate, just like the real Misty had been shipped off to Wayne.

While they are mourning the (fictional) loss of Misty in *Sea Star*, Paul and Maureen find the orphan foal whom Maureen names Sea Star. The meager plot is essentially the attempt on the part of the children and Grandpa to make the starving foal eat. The foal refuses until Grandpa Beebe brings him to a nurse mare owned by a friend, but the family has to trick the grown horse into believing the foal is her own. Grandpa instructs Maureen and Paul to cover the colt with the scent of myrtle, and Grandpa does the same with the mare. The moment the mare decides Sea Star is her baby reads like a poem: *"And then in the middle of a breath came the quiver of sound. It was like a plucked violin string. It was pain and joy and hunger and thirst all mixed into one trembling note. She and the colt were one!"* In the end, both mare and colt come home to the Beebe Ranch. *"Sea Star's come to adopt us!"* says Paul.

The book does contain some truth—there really was an orphan foal that Paul and Maureen discovered, and Misty did star in a film, albeit one produced many years later with a different pony playing her role (the real Misty was too old by then to star as herself). And as with their previous projects together, Marguerite's beautiful prose and Wesley Dennis's art made the story truly resonate. The book was billed as *"continuing the story of Misty"* and *"another wild pony story,"* and it was a big hit.

Sadly, the real colt abandoned by his mother on Chincoteague had an unchronicled life; he did not survive.

Sea Star seemed to be the product of a publisher's wish to keep the "Misty franchise" alive. The writing isn't quite up to the standards of Marguerite's earlier books and the book itself is rather slight. Grandpa Beebe often sounds like a caricature, an exaggerated version of his earlier self. But the portrait of Sea Star splashing through the surf that appeared on the original edition's cover was one of the most beautiful paintings that Dennis made. It held pride of place over the mantel in Marguerite's home in Wayne, and it was one of many of the artist's paintings that she brought with her when she and Sid moved to Rancho Santa Fe, California.

1306 Versailles Road
LEXINGTON, KY

GIBSON WHITE

Thurs., Nov. 3

Dear Marguerite,

What age group will the story
be written for? a title yet?

We had snow today!

Dad is leaving for the Harrisburg Sale
tomorrow, we are selling six and will
probably buy about that many.

Mother spent last week in Orlando.
Bought a home for Dad and herself.
Their address will be 917 N. Westmoreland,
after Nov. 20th.

Our best to Sid and Misty.

Sincerely,
Gib

6

BORN TO TROT

6

"Rosalind and his father were a matched pair.
It was the teamwork that made them great.
The speed in his father's mind flowed through his hands
into her mind. The two even seemed to think alike."

—

FROM *Born to Trot*
(First Published 1950)

The story of Ben Franklin White, one of the greatest trainers of trotting horses in Standardbred racing history, his son Gibson White, and their horse Rosalind marked Marguerite's triumphant return to a real-life story of "a boy and a horse." Theirs was not only another tale of true-life heartbreak and triumph, but it was also the first time that Marguerite attempted a daring, quite inventive idea: creating a book within a book. It was a device inspired by one of Marguerite's librarian friends.

The book "inside" *Born to Trot* is entitled *One Man's Horse*, and *it* was the book that Marguerite wanted to write first, long before she'd ever heard of Ben or Gibson White or their horse.

After writing about Sham, the Godolphin Arabian, the foundational sire of the Thoroughbred breed (flat racing) in *King of the Wind,* Marguerite wanted to do the same for the foundational sire of the Standardbred breed, which had been developed for the sport of harness racing (trotting or pacing while pulling a "sulky"—a two-wheeled lightweight cart).

Early in her research Marguerite discovered a horse known as Rysdyk's Hambletonian was credited as this important stallion in the world of Standardbreds. Marguerite became so carried away by the urgency of the idea of writing about the horse Hambletonian that, by her telling, she dashed straight from her home barn in Wayne to her editor's office in Chicago. When she shared this history, was she embellishing a bit for effect, like when she said she had written almost an entire book in a cemetery? Perhaps. But Marguerite described the moment with dramatic flair. *"On fire with the idea and still wearing my barn boots, I hitchhiked a ride to the city and burst in upon my editor Mary Alice Jones,"* she recalled in "The Story Behind the Story of Born to Trot" in *Dear Readers and Riders.*

Jones wasn't nearly as enthusiastic about the idea as Marguerite had hoped she would be; in fact, Jones had several objections. There was the problem of the two "unpronounceable" names—Hambletonian and Rysdyk—and the fact that the latter was a very old man when his horse Hambletonian finally achieved fame. He wasn't the right sort of hero for a children's book, argued Jones. As Marguerite recounted, her editor's reluctance was specific and general. *"The name Rysdyk's Hambletonian is very cumbrous. It is as awkward as a frying pan with too long a handle,"* said Jones. Furthermore, she said, *"What concerns me even more is that you propose to do a story with no young people at all, and a horse who never won a race."*

These may have seemed like valid points, but Marguerite wasn't quite ready to abandon her idea of a book about the old man and his horse, so she went back to the library and did (more) research. Fortuitously, during this research, a helpful librarian found a magazine article she thought Marguerite might find useful for the book—the story of Ben and Gibson White, the father-and-son team whose mare Rosalind had won the Hambletonian Stakes in 1936. (The Hambletonian, named for the foundational sire of harness horses, is for Standardbreds what the Kentucky Derby is for Thoroughbreds.)

The Gibsons' story intrigued Marguerite, but it was the accompanying picture that convinced her that they could be a great hook for her book. The picture showed a gangly young fellow, with the drawn appearance of someone possibly newly released from the hospital, hugging a genial-looking white-haired man holding the reins. The young man's father had just piloted the mare Rosalind to victory in the Hambletonian. The caption read: *"I've not only a great mare, I have a great dad."* This was such a great line that (naturally) it would have to end up in Marguerite's book.

The "great dad" Ben White won the Hambletonian four times and was a trainer so famous there was even a racetrack in Orlando, Florida, named after him. (The track, Ben White Raceway, has since closed and has been turned into a park.) Ben White had bred and raised Rosalind, and when his son Gibson was languishing in the hospital with tuberculosis (TB), White gave him the filly, hoping to spur his son to a full recovery.

Winning the Hambletonian four times was truly a remarkable feat in the harness racing world; Ben White not only had the stature of a real-life hero but the evident deeply felt bond between father and son was an inspirational story that moved Marguerite. But she still had to figure out how to put the Gibson story together with the tale of Rysdyk's Hambletonian: the old man with the odd name, his horse with the equally challenging name, and the captivating, contemporary story of a sickly young man, his famous father, and a great mare that brought joy to them both and perhaps even helped save the young man's life.

Marguerite was also ripe for a new travel opportunity, and once more urged on by Sid, she journeyed to Lexington, Kentucky, where the Whites kept their training stable, and later to Goshen, New York, where the horse Hambletonian was born and the race named for him was held every year. (The Hambletonian race was later moved to the much larger, much more commercial, and much less charming Meadowlands Racetrack in East Rutherford, New Jersey.) Marguerite also visited the grave of Hambletonian in rural Chester, New York, finding it tucked away in a field, much as it had been left many years earlier. Marguerite traveled to all these locations because she wanted to know the places that the horse and the man Rysdyk had lived while researching her "book within the book" as assiduously as she did the "real" story of the Whites and Rosalind.

The Gibsons welcomed Marguerite into their lives and into their racing and training worlds, so much so that, for a while, Marguerite seemed to be spending as much time on racetracks as she did inside libraries. She had the opportunity to interview some of the legendary drivers and trainers of the time (including S.F. "Sep" Palin, one of the greatest harness horsemen in history), as well as racehorse owners, the president of the Hambletonian Society, and numerous radio announcers and turf writers. Marguerite dove into all the details of harness racing: How did they announce a race? How did the trainers prepare their horses? What did it feel like to drive a horse at a furious trot rather than ride one at a full gallop? There were endless details Marguerite was determined to get right, filling sheets of paper and those manila folders she favored with her notes.

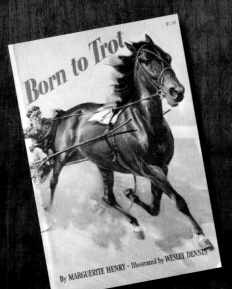

/ 43 /
The original edition cover
for *Born to Trot*
(Rand McNally, 1950).

/ 44 /
This iconic photo of Gibson and Ben White (holding the reins) and
Rosalind after winning The Hambletonian Stakes in 1936 became
the inspiration behind Marguerite's 1950 book *Born to Trot*.

◆ *Photos courtesy of Benny White*

/ 45 /
Marguerite and the
Whites became good
friends after spending
so much time together
while Marguerite was
researching *Born to Trot*.
That necessarily included
time at the track while
Gibson and his father
Ben White were training.
✦ *Photo courtesy of Benny White*

/ 46 /
Marguerite holding Gibson White's young son
Benny's hand as she presented the winner's trophy
to Gibson at a race in Lexington, Kentucky, in 1950.
✦ *Photo courtesy of Benny White*

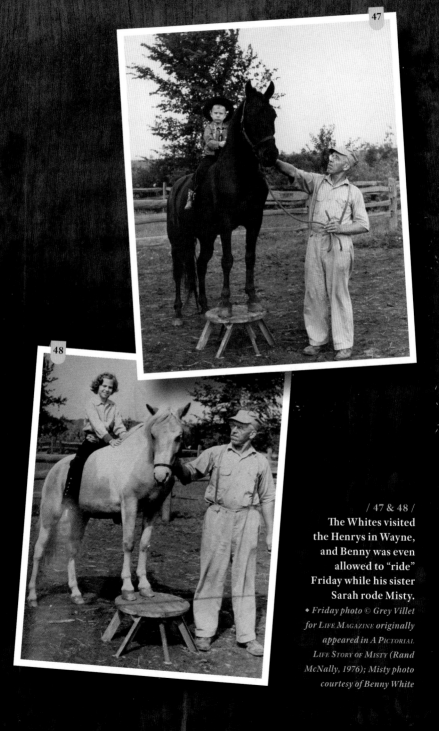

47

48

/ 47 & 48 /
The Whites visited
the Henrys in Wayne,
and Benny was even
allowed to "ride"
Friday while his sister
Sarah rode Misty.

◆ *Friday photo* © *Grey Villet*
for LIFE MAGAZINE *originally*
appeared in A PICTORIAL
LIFE STORY OF MISTY *(Rand*
McNally, 1976); Misty photo
courtesy of Benny White

WESTERN UNION

1950 OCT 26 PM 6 22

SB30 CTB474

CT.LXA519 RX PD=LEXINGTON KY 26 553P=

:MRS MARGUERITE HENRY=

:WAYNE ILL=I

ROSALIND DIED MAYBE MY FAULT COULD NOT VISUALIZE STRONG
ENOUGH=
. GIB=

50

JAMES CAGNEY
BEVERLY HILLS, CALIFORNIA
March 13, 1951

Dear Gib:

Just received your card from California.
Had already read the story and do think it's a very
good job. It was sent me by a friend in New York who
knows of my interest in the harness business. I suggested to the folks out West that they have a look at
it and to let me know if they want to do anything about
it. The trouble is , we have so many stories ahead
already contracted for, that there might be some
delay in considering it. However, they will let me
know, so we'll see what happens.

My very best to you and your Dad, and the
families.

Sincerely,

Jim Cagney

Mr. Gibson White
Route 2
Orlando, Florida

/ 49 & 50 /

The telegram Gibson White sent Marguerite upon Rosalind's passing at
the relatively young age of 16, and the letter from actor James Cagney
telling Gibson of his interest in a film based on *Born to Trot*.

◆ *Image 50 courtesy of Benny White*

Misty's birthday was celebrated at least once
a year by her (many) youthful fans.

51

52

Sid Henry (seen here holding Misty and Friday at home in Wayne)
was game to play groom but Marguerite was the equestrian in the family.

*◆ Photo courtesy of the Marguerite Henry Collection, The Kerlan, University of Minnesota
Archives originally appeared in DEAR READERS AND RIDERS (Rand McNally, 1969)*

53

54

/ 53–55 /

A rare photograph of Marguerite riding Misty (*top left*), as it was far more often a small group of children who climbed aboard—sometimes on authorized rides, and sometimes not. Art Richardson lived on a farm in Wayne not far from Marguerite (*bottom left*) and was one of Misty's first riders. Judy Coffin (*top right*) was another accomplished young equestrian in Wayne who rode Misty from time to time.

♦ Photos © Grey Villet for LIFE MAGAZINE *originally appeared in* A PICTORIAL LIFE STORY OF MISTY *(Rand McNally, 1976)*

55

56

57

/ 56 & 57 /

Alex and "Mom Cat"—and Misty too—were allowed free rein
in the Henry living room. The Wesley Dennis painting of Sea Star
over the fireplace was one of Marguerite's favorites. Misty's
neighborhood friend Eddie Richardson often joined such gatherings.

Marguerite cast a wide
net in her search for just
the right "burro muse"
while writing *Brighty of
the Grand Canyon* in the
early fifties and found
a perfect one in Jiggs,
who fittingly came from
a farm not far from her
own Illinois home.

/ 59 /
When Jiggs arrived at Mole Meadow, he fell in love
with Misty almost immediately. Misty tolerated him.

• *Photo originally appeared in A PICTORIAL LIFE STORY OF MISTY*
(Rand McNally, 1976)

The Book Lady

Perhaps Marguerite's most interesting research was her brief stint in a local sanitorium as a so-called "book lady." Because Gibson White had spent long years while he was a teenager in a sanitorium (possibly in North Carolina, according to Gibson's son Ben, Jr.), Marguerite decided that she should spend time in one too. She wanted to know what it was like to lie in a hospital bed, day after day, not knowing if it was possible to ever get well.

Fortunately, Marguerite lived fairly close to one of the few remaining sanitoriums in the country, so she volunteered to deliver books once a week to the patients of the Naperville Sanitorium (since renamed the Edward Hospital) in Naperville, Illinois. About a half an hour's drive from her home in Wayne, the sanitorium was comprised of a large main house as well as several surrounding cottages where patients lived for months at a time—some even sleeping in tents, as the additional exposure was thought to be good for their health.

Marguerite later explained that she had wanted to understand what it was like to be *"buttoned up in a small space, away from family,"* but also, in some ways, the experience was to remind her of her own early life as an invalid—and how far she had come from those restricted years. *"In writing the part of Gib White, I was, of course, experiencing how I had lived,"* Marguerite said. It was perhaps the most honest and most direct she had been about the difficulties of her childhood illness, which she had mostly described to her young readers in vague, almost pleasant terms. But it had clearly left a mark in ways that Marguerite rarely mentioned.

Marguerite's description of life in a sanitorium in *Born to Trot* was in accordance with the life of a TB patient described in *The Pantagraph* (November 9, 1947) of Bloomington, Illinois. Residents of the sanitorium were subjected to a *"minimum of seven months bed rest"* for a *"minimal"* case of TB and sometimes they might later be allowed to swing their legs over a bed and sit up. *"As you improve you are allowed one bathroom privilege, which builds up eventually to full bathroom privileges plus taking meals out of bed."* And such privileges were gender specific. Men could take their meals with other men while female TB patients—for some unstated reason—were constrained to dine alone, albeit on a private "sun porch."

The Naperville Sanitorium had been founded by Eudora Gaylord Spalding in 1907 after her first husband died of TB, and it remained one of the leading tuberculosis sanitoriums in the country until 1955, when it was converted into a hospital. Tuberculosis was such a scourge in the early twentieth century that in 1900 in Chicago, one in five hundred people died of it. But thanks to advances in modern medicine, hospitals strictly devoted to tuberculosis patients were no longer necessary less than sixty years later. (A local paper noted that the first patient of the sanitorium-turned-hospital was a boy who had been kicked by a horse.)

Marguerite's stint as a sanitorium book lady helped her create a physical world in which she could connect the story of Rysdyk's Hambletonian to that of Rosalind and the Whites. Marguerite reasoned that since Gibson, spending months in bed recovering from his illness, would be avid to read books, especially books about horses, *"One of them could be about Hambletonian."* The story within a story, *One Man's Horse,* was so convincing that readers of *Born to Trot* asked Marguerite where they might buy *One Man's Horse.*

Marguerite interspersed the chapters of *One Man's Horse* with the chapters of the book about Gibson White's life. *One Man's Horse* begins when White starts to read the book and ends when he closes a chapter. *"With his finger marking the picture, Gibson looked up a moment at his bulletin board as if to make sure of Rosalind. Satisfied, he let the book fall open again,"* Marguerite wrote. A few paragraphs later, both Gibson White and the reader are back into the story of Rysdyk once more. The different typefaces used for the book's chapters—differentiating between the "inside book" and the "real book"—are an additional cue for the reader.

Marguerite oddly made no mention of Hambletonian's longtime Black/Native American groom Harmon Fink Showers in *Born to Trot,* though Showers was utterly devoted to both Hambletonian and William Rysdyk for many years. When the latter became bedridden, Showers walked Hambletonian past Rysdyk's house every day so he might see his horse and speak to him, and when Hambletonian died in 1876, the local paper reported that Showers—*"an aged colored man"*—refused to be comforted.

Secret Notetaker

When she wasn't handing out books at the sanitorium, Marguerite was following Ben and Gibson White on the racing circuit. She didn't know anything about harness racing; she'd only witnessed and researched Thoroughbred (flat) racing. There was a great deal to learn as harness racing was an entirely different world from the one in which she'd immersed herself to write *King of the Wind,* Marguerite noted. There was not only the complexity of the racing style, there was the gear (harnessing a Standardbred racehorse is a great deal more complicated, and time-consuming, than simply saddling a horse up).

Marguerite described an early morning she spent at the The Red Mile track in Lexington, Kentucky, in *Dear Readers and Riders*: "*The first horses were skimming the track—three times the wrong way, three times the right way, spinning faster and faster with each mile. In the deserted stands a few owners and trainers were clustered at the rail, clocking their horses. I stood within earshot, trying to feel how it would be to own a big-going trotter; better still to drive one!"*

Marguerite took notes at the track secretly, scratching away with her pencil onto bits of paper she'd tucked in her pockets. She wrote without looking at the notes as she was writing them, furtive as an undercover journalist on a stakeout. It's an interesting image and an interesting admission on Marguerite's part—why would she feel the need to keep her notes secret? Marguerite never explained why she didn't want the trainers and drivers to know that she was eavesdropping on their conversations.

During one of these furtive note-taking mornings, Marguerite overheard a man at the rail watching a filly during a workout exclaim, *"She was born to trot!"*

And with that, Marguerite had the name for her book.

How true to life was the story in *Born to Trot*? According to Ben White, Jr., son of Gibson White (who goes by "Benny") and a racehorse trainer himself, now retired and living in Florida, Marguerite got a great deal of the story and the details of racing right. For example, the scene in *Born to Trot* where Gibson has to jump on the back of a runaway horse after the rein breaks while he is driving actually happened, his son confirmed. At the time, there were a number of newspaper stories about the accident and Gibson White's remarkable feat, although Marguerite had changed a seemingly minor fact. It was not Gibson White's first race, although Marguerite described it as such. Perhaps she had decided it should be his first to heighten the drama?

As for Gibson White's stint in the sanitorium, it lasted even longer than Marguerite's book suggested, said his son. "I think he [his father

Gibson] went in when he was about sixteen, and it was about three or four years until he got out," Ben Jr. recalled. But, Ben Jr. noted, it was very much the truth that his father had been released just before the Hambletonian race so he could watch his father, Ben Sr., drive Rosalind to record-breaking victory in 1936.

It wasn't an entirely happy ending in real life. Gibson White soon had a relapse and had to go back to the sanitorium for a few months. But there was a bonus (that did not appear in the book): Gibson met Emily, a nurse at the sanitorium, and she became his wife.

Like Marguerite, Wesley Dennis became good friends with the Whites and spent a great deal of time with them at their farm in Lexington, sketching Rosalind and the other horses on the track. He later sent the Whites a painting from in his studio in Buzzards Bay, Massachusetts, as a gesture of goodwill. Ben White Jr., who has the painting displayed in his house today, said he was a bit puzzled by the subject— the painting isn't of Rosalind, or for that matter, a horse at all, but a lobsterman with lobster traps. Why did a man famous for painting horses give a picture of a lobsterman to a trainer of horses? Was it one of the practical jokes for which Dennis was famous? Perhaps it was— or perhaps not. Ben White Jr. prizes it all the same.

Moving Actors to Tears

A year after *Born to Trot* was published, Gibson White was contacted by the actor James Cagney (whose films include *White Heat,* among many others), who was a fan of the book, and harness racing as well. Harness racing was as popular as Thoroughbred racing in those days, and the sport attracted quite a few famous fans. In a letter dated March 13, 1951, Cagney wrote that he had read *Born to Trot,* which he described as *"a very good job,"* and that he'd suggested to *"the folks out*

West" (aka Hollywood) that they *"have a look at it and let me know if they want to do anything about it."*

Three-time-Oscar-nominated actor Charles Coburn wrote a letter to Gibson White that same week—he was equally impressed by Marguerite's book. Coburn described his response in emotional terms: *"I am greatly indebted to you for* Born to Trot—*a magnificent story, beautifully told by Margaret (sic) Henry and exquisitely illustrated by Wesley Dennis. I enjoyed every minute of it and I am not ashamed to confess that I had a good cry several times while reading your story."*

Coburn also believed that the Whites' story would make a terrific movie; he even suggested himself for the part of Ben White. Coburn explained that he and his late wife had fallen in love while performing *As You Like It* when she happened to be playing the part of Rosalind, so the filly's name seemed prophetic to him and further proof that the part should be his if a movie were made. Coburn added a poignant note about his wife: *"We were together thirty-two years, and her passing was a terrific loss to me, as you can well imagine."* (Ivah Wills Coburn died at the age of 58 in 1937.) How many other children's books have inspired intimate confessions from famous actors and moved them to tears?

(Coburn's fear that it might be difficult to convince a studio to make a film from the book proved well-founded; *Born to Trot* was never made into a movie. However, Coburn remained a horse lover for the rest of his life, and he even had a young filly of his own that he hoped would turn out to be a top harness racehorse. He named her Ivah C, in an homage to his late wife.)

Legacies Forgotten—and Those Remembered

Gibson White died in 1972 just before Rosalind was inducted into the Harness Racing Hall of Fame. As for Rosalind? She only lived to be sixteen years old after having six foals, all fillies, none of whom repeated their dam's remarkable feat. "She held the world record for thirty-eight years," Ben White Jr. recalled, although he acknowledged that her winning time would be much less impressive by today's much faster standards. "The breed is getting faster and faster. If a minute fifty-six was as fast as she could go, that won't get you much today," he said. In fact, he added a rather depressing footnote: "Rosalind would be a three-thousand-dollar claiming horse today." (A claiming race is one in which all the horses running are for sale at a set price; a price of three thousand dollars is quite low.)

When Rosalind died, Gibson White sent Marguerite a Western Union telegram dated October 26, 1950, with this poignant message:

ROSALIND DIED MAYBE MY FAULT COULD NOT
VISUALIZE STRONG ENOUGH.

It was signed *"Gib."*

Perhaps the combination of her early death and comparatively slow speed is why Rosalind is oddly unmentioned in the Harness Racing Hall of Fame today. There is, however, a very large display devoted to Greyhound, the gelding who raced at the same time that Rosalind did and was spoken of as her male counterpart. But so much has changed from the harness world of Rosalind's day when Hollywood stars wanted to make movies about them and readers wrote Marguerite, asking how to visit the place where Hambletonian was born. Harness racing today is a nearly forgotten sport, and the track in Goshen, New York, a wonderful throwback to another era, is only utilized once a year in July when the faithful—and the nostalgic—turn out in large numbers to watch the Standardbreds turn round its oval once more.

As to the readers who wrote her, asking if they might visit Hambletonian's grave, Marguerite answered them all. When a young reader named Pattie Ross asked whether she would be able to find the grave marker of the great trotting horse, Marguerite gave her detailed directions that sounded more like the words found in a fairytale: *"You will pass the tiny post office, the lace maker, the wood carver, and the candle maker. Don't stop at them now but drive ahead to the little white country church. Just this side of it, turn right onto Pine Hill Road and wind up and up to a fork. Take the left 'tine,' marked 'Hambletonian Road' going past a few scattered houses until you come to Hambletonian Birthplace Farm owned by T. Wakely Bankers. Anyone about the place will show you the way to a log footbridge and just beyond it is your destination!"*

With this detailed response Marguerite may have been imagining herself as young Pattie, so taken with the story of Gibson White and Hambletonian that she had to travel from Illinois to New York to see the marker of the great horse with her own eyes. A curious mind who needed to see where and how a story unfolded, for herself. (Surprisingly, Marguerite's directions are mostly still valid: there may not be a wood carver or candlemaker in Sugar Loaf Village but there is a shop *selling* candles. The marker in the pasture has been moved to the side of Hambletonian Road, a hundred or so yards from the site of the horse's actual birth, rather than where he was eventually buried. It is still there for those who remember and love the sport and *Born to Trot*.)

And the great horse's owner? The house that Hambletonian enabled Rysdyk to buy still stands in Chester, New York, arguably the grandest house in that small town, and Hambletonian's name is duly noted there as well. But Rysdyk himself reposes in an unmarked grave in an overgrown field outside the town. While his horse has been long honored after death, the man's contribution seems largely forgotten. (It seems likely Rysdyk would be all right with that fact.)

The publication of *Born to Trot* was timed to the Kentucky Futurity at the Trots race that took place in the fall of 1950. It was a boon to Marguerite's book signings that they were not only announced in the book pages of newspapers but oftentimes in the sports pages as well. And it helped even more that Marguerite and Gibson White did many of the book signings together. *"Marguerite Henry will be in Carson's Hobby Horse Book Shop.... And Gibson White—the principal character in her new story—will be there, too!"* noted an ad in *The Chicago Tribune* that year. Marguerite had the great good fortune to have traded a cute pony sidekick for a young man with a winning true-life tale of terrible heartbreak turned impossible victory, and unlike *Misty of Chincoteague,* the story of Gibson White was almost entirely true.

Chicago Tribune "Front Views and Profile" columnist Lucy Key Miller wrote that Marguerite and Gibson—whom she described as *"looking like Hoagy Carmichael"*— read a chapter aloud from the book at the signing. And when Marguerite was asked how long it took her to write the book, she had ready a snappy reply: *"The same length of time it takes to foal a colt—eleven months."* (Marguerite used that line many, many times when queried about the length of time it took her to write her books. It may not have always been accurate, but it sounded good.)

Born to Trot earned rave reviews from book critics. *The Omaha World Herald* called it *"perhaps the best junior book on trotting horses ever written"* (December 10, 1950), while *The Sheboygan Press* (Wisconsin) predicted the book, *"filled with dramatic action...will bring new thrills to boys and girls"* (November 15, 1950), and Leigh Tucker, a columnist for the *Orlando Evening Star,* profiled Marguerite during her Florida book tour and described the book in glowing terms in her column published April 10, 1950: "Born to Trot *will join the growing list of best-loved books on the shelves of children's libraries of the country."* Dennis was on hand for the book tour, drawing pictures of the people and horses alike, noted Tucker, and Marguerite and Dennis produced a radio play based on the book for an Orlando children's radio show.

The year *Born to Trot* was published was a particularly propitious one for horse-themed children's books. According to a piece published in *The Standard-Star* of New Rochelle, New York, no fewer than fourteen books published that year featured horses as the main characters, and sales of *King of the Wind* and *Sea Star* totaled an impressive one hundred and forty-six thousand copies. (By comparison, for a children's book considered to be "successful" in those days it might sell ten to twenty thousand.) Marguerite's sales numbers made her a superstar.

Marguerite remained a fan of harness racing long after *Born to Trot* was published, but she made it clear that her affection was for the trotters (horses whose legs move in diagonal pairs), not the pacers (whose legs move laterally—right front and right hind together, left front and left hind together). As she wrote to a friend many decades later (1988), *"I love the trotters. They are beautiful and free in action. But when the pacers come out in full gear with hobbles etcetera, they remind me of a hospital patient working their hearts out in rehabilitation."* Because pacers are likely to break stride, they invariably must wear the confining hobbles that Marguerite so disliked. (Anyone who has watched a pacer in a race will realize Marguerite described their actions exactly right.)

Marguerite maintained a friendship with the White family for many years. Mrs. White was particularly happy to visit Marguerite and not talk about the horses that dominated her life. *"She never fails to say the best time of her entire life was her few days in Wayne listening to lady fripperies instead of colic, cribbing and quarter cracks,"* Marguerite wrote. ("Colic" is a gastrointestinal problem and common killer of horses; "cribbing" is when a horse chews on walls and fences; and "quarter cracks" in the hooves are a frequent problem among race-horses and can cause lameness.)

Today, *Born to Trot* lives on in the form of Ben White, Jr., who, now seventy-seven years of age, has retired from training and driving race-horses ("After being on the road for so long, you want to be home"). He still hears from readers of *Born to Trot* and happily fields requests for his autograph on their copies of the book.

letters

MARGUERITE HENRY

A dull bronze day
in November

Dearest Gee Gee,

How I love your "Lonely Sorrel"!   It
begins sad and mournful, becomes joyful and happy,
and has a nice denouement, explaining God's way in
the world. You have presented your thoughts with
skill.

How can I can criticize? The poem is so quiet
and smooth, it conveys its thoughts so clearly. Only
word I think you could change, and that is "whine."
One
I'm so eager to see you!

'Til then

best love,

Marguerite (Mom II)

BRIGHTY
OF THE GRAND CANYON

7

"Was there a wildness in Brighty that could never be tamed?
A need for freedom stronger than the need for companionship?"

—

FROM *BRIGHTY OF THE GRAND CANYON*
(FIRST PUBLISHED 1953)

When Marguerite had the stable built behind her house with "Misty money," she directed it to be built it for three horses—although at the time she had only two. She must have been prescient, as just a few years after Friday arrived, Marguerite added a burro (aka donkey—the term "burro" is commonly used for the smaller or wild version of the species). This burro soon became a favorite among the local children, especially Sidney "Tex" Drexler, who had already established himself as one of Marguerite's favorites. Indeed, in his 2016 obituary, Drexler was noted as having "worked for famed author Marguerite Henry" when he was eight years old.

Marguerite's burro came with the name Jiggs. As Misty had been a "pony muse" for Marguerite when she was writing *Misty of Chincoteague,* so Jiggs became the stand-in for Brighty, the hero of Marguerite's next, beloved tale about a real-life burro who wandered around the Grand Canyon at the turn of the twentieth century, and who may or may not have helped solve a murder.

Inspired by a Free Spirit

The idea for *Brighty* was first floated to Marguerite by Mildred Lathrop, a librarian in Elgin, Illinois, who had helped Marguerite with the research for several of her books, including *Album of Horses,* a reference about breeds of horses and their origins published in 1950, the same year as *Born to Trot.* Marguerite had developed a curiosity about burros during the course of her research for the *Album*—she learned how different they were from horses, and how in many ways they were even harder to know. For example, Marguerite learned that a burro was far more intelligent than a horse, more reliable, and less skittish. While a horse's first reaction in many frightening instances is most often to flee, a burro might stand still and think. It is this thinking that has often been misconstrued as stubbornness.

Marguerite and Dennis shared a love of burros. In an interview in the *Chicago Tribune,* Marguerite enumerated the three qualities they liked best about small-but-mighty donkeys: *"a rollicking sense of humor, a willingness to work, but a passionate distaste for overwork."* That seemed like a smart summing-up of burro character—and particularly Brighty, the hero of her newest book.

Lathrop had read about the burro named Bright Angel who lived in the Grand Canyon for a couple of decades in a story published in *Sunset* magazine in 1922, and she passed the magazine along to

Marguerite. Written by Thomas McKee, whose father-in-law ran the Wylie Way Camp near Bright Angel Point of the Grand Canyon when Brighty was still alive, the article told of Brighty's discovery and life. According to McKee, cowboys had been commissioned to look for a man from Chicago who had vanished somewhere in the Grand Canyon. They didn't find the man, but they found Brighty at a campsite, just "hanging around." And that was where the story of the free-spirited burro began.

By McKee's telling, Brighty roamed the canyon freely, occasionally being put to work (if, in fact, he deigned to oblige) by cowboys in the canyon. Brighty, he wrote, occasionally befriended people, some of whom were famous, including (possibly) President Theodore Roosevelt. According to McKee, his own son Bob was one of the people Brighty allowed to press him into service occasionally—mostly carrying saddle bags filled with water up and down the canyon paths.

A Real-Life Adventure

Although Brighty was no longer alive when Marguerite read the article, she thought it had the earmarks of a story that might be turned into a book. This meant doing the necessary research—aka traveling to the Grand Canyon to follow the paths that Brighty trod—to get an understanding of the place and what had been his life.

Marguerite chose to undertake the outing in the middle of winter, and later admitted she would not have gone on the trip at all if she'd had to travel to Arizona alone—she wouldn't have been brave enough. There was the challenge of the weather, and the challenge of the trail itself. But Sid was game to accompany her, and his was a particularly stalwart offer since Marguerite didn't know until the end of their adventure that Sid suffered from acrophobia (fear of heights). A trip up and down the canyon on thirty-two-inch-wide canyon trails on the back of a mule, following Brighty's path, terrified Sid—although he didn't admit that to Marguerite until after they had safely made the trip down the canyon and back up again. (Mules are the resulting offspring of a male donkey and female horse and have long been the choice of canyon guides owing to their surefootedness and size—they are usually much larger than burros. They are also quite brave. Stories abound of mules attacking and killing mountain lions—some true, some fiction.)

It was an adventure with a real element of peril; just prior to their journey, Sid visited a supply store near the Grand Canyon to buy some warm clothing for their trail ride, including long underwear. While there he overheard the store's proprietor discussing two local guides who'd recently fallen off the trail to their deaths. Sid didn't mention this fact to Marguerite until much later—long after their trip was concluded.

It was Valentine's Day week, with February temperatures of a frosty six degrees, and the trails were covered with snow. Marguerite was nervous, but she later wrote that when their guide gave her the mailbag to carry behind her saddle, she felt relieved, reasoning that if the mail could make it down the canyon wall—as it had time and time again—then surely she (and Sid) would survive the experience as well.

Their destination was Phantom Ranch, the only overnight accommodations offered below the rim of the Canyon, and then, as now, the lodge could only be reached by foot or muleback or raft. Marguerite took notes, interviewing guides and "mule skinners" (people who specialize in handling mules) while they made their way down. Sid rode behind Marguerite, and unbeknownst to her, was hanging on for dear life. Marguerite only realized the depth of Sid's terror when they ascended to the canyon rim the following day and Sid threw his arms around his mule (called Boob) and gave him a kiss for delivering Sid from what had seemed (to him) certain death.

Marguerite made return trips to the Grand Canyon and even spent the night in a cave as she understood the real Brighty had—although she was apprised of the possibility of certain visitors. In a letter to a young reader named Brian Mitchener who wrote Marguerite, wondering how the story of Brighty came about and if everything she described had actually happened, she replied in great detail, including this note: *"The park rangers warned me to listen to a soft, whimpering cry like a baby's. 'That will be a mountain lion,' they said. 'But if you lie motionless he will not harm you.'"* Sure enough, the mountain lion came by, breathing just as park rangers predicted, and although Marguerite wanted to look, she was too scared, and burrowed even deeper into her sleeping bag. (She did not mention Sid in records of this account, but it's hard to believe he wasn't right beside Marguerite, scrunched down inside his own sleeping bag.)

Enter: Jiggs

Marguerite set out to find a Brighty stand-in to serve as her model and inspiration. *"I can't write about an animal character unless he's part of our establishment,"* Marguerite explained in an essay in *The Chicago Tribune* (November 15, 1953). It wasn't just the look of the creature that she needed but the smell and feel as well. To write about Brighty, Marguerite wanted to be able to run her hand through the burro's coat and *"look deep into his almond eyes,"* she said.

It seemed like a simple enough quest. Marguerite sent word out to various local farmers and even contacted the director of Chicago's Brookfield Zoo about her burro search, and each one, in turn, helpfully supplied her with the names of farmers with donkeys. Marguerite "interviewed" several of them (the burros, not the farmers) but none seemed quite right. Marguerite had a very particular muse in mind; she described the burro she wanted like another woman might the man of her dreams. Her burro had to have *"busy ears and great brown eyes and a watershed of hair over the eyes to give him a sweet, unkempt look."* It seemed like a dauntingly specific list, but eventually Marguerite found just the right candidate: a burro named Jiggs from a village with the perfectly magical name of Sugar Grove (not far from Naperville, Marguerite's former home).

Much like Misty and the friendly agreement Marguerite had with Grandpa Beebe, Jiggs was initially "on loan"; Marguerite paid his owner twenty-five dollars a month, with the agreement that she might keep the donkey up to a year. (She later purchased him.) Jiggs quickly fell in love with Misty, but reportedly, the feeling was not returned. Misty was far more interested in human attention and snacks than a burro's affections, said Marguerite, although Jiggs never stopped trying to convince Misty otherwise. *"If Misty goes to a school for the day he brays and sobs,"* Marguerite told a reporter from *The Chicago Tribune.*

Neighbor boy Sid "Tex" Drexler, on the other hand, was crazy about Jiggs, and the two soon formed a fast partnership, riding along with Marguerite on Friday and Ed Richardson on Misty some three days a week. On the days that the trio didn't ride together, Marguerite sometimes rode Friday with a group of neighborhood women along the trails. They filled their saddlebags with wildflower seeds, scattering them as they went so that flowers might one day bloom in their wake.

Jiggs proved not only an exceptional book model but also a capable actor (he later starred in the *Brighty of the Grand Canyon* film that was produced in 1966, starring famed American actor Joseph Cotten). He was such a perfect model that Wesley Dennis traveled to Wayne to sketch Jiggs for the book—never mind that there were burros in Virginia too. Marguerite made note of his degree of artistic devotion: *"Wesley spent an entire day in our pasture making sketches of Jiggs, our winsome little burro who struck a gay variety of poses,"* she said.

As Marguerite noted in the *Something About the Author* book series (*Volume 7*), Dennis and she often visited one another while working on a book together. They exchanged phone calls and letters too, but their in-person encounters seemed essential, far beyond a sort of practical meeting between writer and artist. *"With Wesley Dennis either he would come to my home in the plains of Illinois, or I would go to his in the mountains of Virginia and then we would read aloud the first rough draft. I loved this day above others for I had always wanted to be an actress and I could dramatize the story with all the ham actor in my soul,"* Marguerite said. Wesley would interject, saying a certain scene that Marguerite had written seemed like a good moment for an illustration, and then they each would return home to finish their respective work.

Although in Marguerite's telling of his life, the fictional Brighty faced danger and hardship, some aspects of the real Brighty's life were cleaned up and others omitted, including the sad and sordid facts of his death. The ending of Marguerite's *Brighty* is joyous: *"It seemed all at once that he was free—no one was gripping his tail or prodding him with a rifle and no walls were hemming him in. The wide, free world and the sky above were his."* The epilogue is yet more poetic: *"Everyone knows that Brighty has long since left this earth. But some animals, like some men, leave a trail of glory behind. They give their spirit to the place where they have lived and remain forever a part of the rocks and streams and the wind and sky."*

In reality, Brighty was killed and eaten by two snowbound men one winter—a much less noble end for the legendary burro, and a fate not unlike the fate of many of Brighty's brethren. In fact, from the time of Brighty's death up until the 1970s, thousands of canyon-dwelling donkeys were deliberately slaughtered by the National Parks Service (NPS), who deemed the animals an "invasive" species and detrimental to the native wildlife. The government's reasoning was that donkeys had been brought to the Grand Canyon by prospectors seeking gold, only to be abandoned there when President Theodore Roosevelt turned the Grand Canyon into a National Park. It wasn't until 1971 and the passage by Congress of the Free Roaming Horses and Burros Act that the donkeys in the Canyon were protected, except, of course, by that time all of them had been eradicated from the National Park. While the message of Marguerite's *Brighty* was a character meant to be *"the symbol of the ever-free America,"* according to a reviewer in *The Ludington Daily News* (Michigan), it was not necessarily the truth of the real Brighty's life.

When Marguerite and Sid moved to California years later, Marguerite gave Jiggs to his devoted friend Tex Drexler. Jiggs remained with Drexler until the burro's death in 1974.

letters

MISTY

Dear Peter –

I too like the cat on P. 147 of KING!
His tail upflung makes him more
interesting. He was a tiger tomcat,
marked more like Morris (than
splotched like a female cat).

    Enclosed are more clips &
comments.

    Thoughts and prayers winging
    to you

        Best
          M.

CINNABAR,
THE ONE O'CLOCK FOX

8

"Cinnabar was a big, red magnificent fellow.
Courage and heart showed in the very look of him.
A rough scar across his nose and a nick on one ear in no way
marred his handsomeness. On the contrary,
they gave him a gay and gallant air. They spoke of battles
won—over eagles and buzzards and hawks and weasels."

—

FROM *Cinnabar, The One O'Clock Fox*
(First Published 1956)

Marguerite often said that *Cinnabar, The One O'Clock Fox* was her favorite book. It was the most fun, and it was certainly one of the easiest to write. As Marguerite explained, *"It's pure fiction,"* adding that she didn't have to conduct interviews or fact-check her sources or travel to faraway places to write it. She could simply observe a group of foxes outside her house and *"listen to them as they talked and sang their mystical gibberish to the moon,"* as Marguerite wrote in the piece referenced earlier in these pages entitled "Twenty Questions and Answers."

Furthermore, Marguerite added, perhaps a bit rankled by the challenges that had been posed by the characters in her books who were actual, real people with particular wishes: *"I knew that when it was done I wouldn't have to ask Cinnabar or his vixen or his cubs to read it very carefully and sign a paper saying they approved every word I had written about them."*

A Legend from the Hunt Field

The story of Cinnabar came to Marguerite by way of Dorothy, Wesley Dennis's second wife. Dorothy, an avid fox hunter, told Marguerite the legend of a wily fox who lived during the time of George Washington and who regularly—and promptly—showed up at one o'clock in the afternoon for the president's "fox chases." The book Marguerite would write about him marks a break from her usual style as she describes Cinnabar in anthropomorphic terms. The fox and his mate Vicky live in a den decorated with furniture and books. Their conversations are like those of a human husband and wife, and Cinnabar dotes on his cubs like a human father. There is little that's foxlike about Cinnabar, save for the fact he likes to run and doesn't trust humans.

Marguerite set the stage for action when Cinnabar reads a card that falls out of a huntsman's pocket: *"Weather permitting, our first fall fox chase will be on Saturday next. Gather at Honey Hill at half after ten o'clock."* The card is signed *G. Washington, MFH.* Vicky urges Cinnabar to join the hunt, knowing it may mean his death but also knowing it is an irresistible game to Cinnabar: *"He thought with pleasure that he was the center and object of the whole hunt. He had much to do. And now he must stop daydreaming and do it."* And so the fox is off to join the chase—which he may or may not survive.

In the story, Marguerite captures the feeling of joy Cinnabar finds in running—although Cinnabar delights in "outfoxing" the humans, he is, of course, running for his life too. It's an important point that is treated as a bit of an aside. Did Marguerite feel Cinnabar's detachment about his possible death, or was she deliberately keeping the plot light?

Marguerite even managed to find some fox cubs to serve as her inspiration for Cinnabar, as she had with Misty and Brighty. She'd been trying to figure how to write a book about a fox who could tell time when, providentially, a Wayne neighbor phoned to tell her that he'd found a litter of cubs in a drainpipe nearby. Perhaps Marguerite would want to rescue them, he suggested, without realizing that Marguerite, in fact, was in search of fox models for her book. Marguerite threw on her coat and rushed over to her neighbor's house to borrow a wire-and-wood cage. It helped that this neighbor, George Wood, was then the Joint Master of the Wayne-DuPage Hunt and happened to have just the right sort of cage to hold her fox models.

Marguerite kept the cubs in her backyard in Wayne just outside her living room window, all the better to study them in their cage as they grew. If that seems a bit cruel, Marguerite did pledge that after *Cinnabar* was published, she would set the cubs free, which she did, although she also sent one cub by way of a friend to Dennis in Virginia. Upon arrival on Dennis's farm, the fox promptly escaped.

Marguerite acknowledged many people for their help with her research for *Cinnabar* on the book's back page. She thanked the usual number of librarians as well as a couple of Wayne huntsmen and even a music director—R. Gordon Hinners of St. Charles, Illinois, who helped her with the book's fox hunting songs. Marguerite includes both words and music for such songs: *"Few sportsmen so gallant, if an-y/Did cubs ever send to the chase/Each dingle for him has a cran-ny,"* the sportsmen sing, while Cinnabar has a few songs of his own, although the lyrics don't quite match the light-hearted images of Wesley Dennis's dancing foxes: *"Four little cubs, out on a spree/One found a rabbit trap. Then there were three!"*

"Whoever Finds This—I Love You"

The book was warmly received by reviewers who found it *"a delightful tale... [of a] happy fox family"* and the illustrations particularly winsome. *"Beautifully written, thrilling to read"* wrote a reviewer in the *Wichita Falls Times* (December 16, 1956) who even included a quote from Marguerite, suggesting Cinnabar himself was a patriot and symbol of American freedom: *"'The spirit of a people who fought for freedom and lived for freedom's sake.'"* (The reviewer further suggested, in an interesting and perhaps sexist twist, that the book would be best enjoyed by boys who were between eight and twelve years old. Were girls less susceptible to the charms of a story about foxes, and if so, why?)

Some reviews of the book were not just about the story or prose but noted where and how the book had been written, asides that underscore the celebrity of the author. It wasn't enough that Marguerite had written an admirable book—the story *behind* the book, or at least, the place where the book had been conceived, was even worthy of a mention, it seemed. One unnamed reviewer in *The Sun Tattler* (Nov 15, 1956) of Hollywood, Florida, indicated that Marguerite had written the book while visiting her brother Fred Breithaupt. And, as if to verify this fact, the paper even printed her brother Fred's address: 1235 Jefferson Street in Hollywood. (A rather modest ranch house surrounded by palm trees, it was one of several Florida addresses to which the Breithaupt family decamped during the long Milwaukee winters.) Fred was interviewed about his sister's stay; he communicated that while she was visiting Hollywood, Marguerite made great use of the local library. As to *how* she wrote the book, Fred helpfully explained *"she either dictates her stories to a stenographer or writes them in longhand."* The typist in question for *Cinnabar* was W.R. Bean, a neighbor of Fred's whose address was noted as 1247 Jefferson.

A year later, *The Sun Tattler* reported a talk by Marguerite at the Hollywood Woman's Club (Feb 18, 1957) and printed highlights of her remarks, which included an interesting tidbit about how she viewed herself a writer. Marguerite said she compared herself to an orphan who ties a note to the top of a tree that reads, *"Whoever finds this—I love you."* And any child who was reading one of her books was a child whom *she* loved. This was a statement that must have been well-received as Marguerite repeated it in subsequent interviews.

Marguerite received many letters from readers about *Cinnabar*— commonly wondering if the lead character was a real fox and if George Washington had truly hunted for him—but one particularly interesting query came many years after the book was published, from an adult. William Harper of Cullman, Alabama, wrote to tell Marguerite that he had been so taken with Cinnabar's story that he had been inspired to write a narrative of his own. Harper's letter to Marguerite, dated March 1, 1983, noted that it was actually his second note to her, and was in response to a reply that Marguerite had written him upon receipt of the first. *"I'm surprised that I am the only person that you know to have read Cinnabar as an adult,"* Harper wrote. He confessed that he felt self-conscious about checking a children's book out of the library, but decided not to worry what others might think. He wondered if Marguerite felt self-conscious as well. *"Do such attitudes ever cause a problem for you, being a children's book author?"* he asked. Harper sent Marguerite the story he had written along with a note: *"If upon reading it you find it means something to you that will help even up a debt I and many other readers owe you."*

Alas, there is no record as to whether Harper's story (a tale of talking trees in a forest) was ever published, or what Marguerite thought of it.

letters

To Arthur and Eddie
who know and have
ridden Misty.
    Best wishes
        Marguerite Henry

Dear Blackie — I'd like to meet you!
                    Little-or-Nothing

9

BLACK GOLD

9

*"As the sun bulged over the horizon, other horses and riders
began to grow out of the morning mist. Black Gold's quick ears
caught the drumming of their hoofs and the deep snorting
of their breath, but he ran on, light and easy, heeding nothing
but the fine hands and the warm voice of the boy on his back."*

—

FROM *BLACK GOLD*

(FIRST PUBLISHED 1957)

After her detour into the world of foxes who held human-seeming conversations and possessed human habits, Marguerite returned to the world she knew and chronicled best: horses and heartbreak. The story of Black Gold was perhaps the most tragic that she had written to date—even more so than *King of the Wind*.

Black Gold was one of many famous racehorses that Marguerite had considered for a book; she kept file upon file about Thoroughbreds whose lives might be suitable for a story. She considered Messenger, the stallion imported from England to the United States after the American Revolution, and the great Eclipse, the undefeated British

Thoroughbred from the eighteenth century. (Marguerite pondered the possibility of a book about Eclipse for several decades before finally giving up.) The idea for a book about Black Gold came from a Dennis family friend named Timmie Stephenson from Warrenton, Virginia, who thought the story was well suited to the work of Wesley Dennis and Marguerite.

Samuel D. Riddle, the owner of Man o' War, was also a great admirer of Black Gold, whom he regarded as one of the greatest racehorses in history. *"This little ebony horse, with a young Irish jockey, won the Kentucky Derby in 1924. But that is not what made him great. His best race was his last when with a foreleg broken, he finished on three legs and a heart,"* Mr. Riddle said to Marguerite when she asked him what he thought of the horse.

For Marguerite, the tale of Black Gold held the right combination of triumph and sorrow, and as with *Born to Trot,* it was also a simple tale of a boy who loved a horse. There are two stories in *Black Gold*—the boy's and the horse's—before the two meet. It's a variation of the "story within a story technique" that Marguerite employed with *Born to Trot,* although in this case, the characters' stories unfolded over the same period. But unlike the White family's contribution to the research Marguerite did for *Born to Trot,* the most important characters around the story of Black Gold were either long dead or did not want to talk.

Rosa Captain Hoots, the owner of Black Gold and the widow of Al (Alfred) Hoots, whose dream had been to breed a great racehorse, were both dead, as was Black Gold's trainer Hanley Webb—the man most people held responsible for the colt's death. Al Hoots passed away before Black Gold was born, and Rosa Hoots died in 1938 at seventy years old, decades before Marguerite began her research. Hoots's obituary made no mention of Black Gold's tragic death, merely noting that he had *"died several years ago"* but that for many years, Rosa Hoots had kept a portrait of Black Gold above the mantel in her house.

Black Gold's jockey, Jaydee (John D.) Mooney (aka "Sit Still Mooney") was alive when Marguerite began writing, but he had no intention of talking with her; it was said the horse's death weighed heavily upon him. But with her customary mix of both charm and doggedness, Marguerite followed Jaydee and his wife Marjorie to racetracks in New York and Kentucky, trying to persuade them to participate in her story, assuring them that her book would reveal the truth of Black Gold's life—and of Jaydee's deep love for the horse. She hung around Aqueduct, the gritty racetrack in the borough of Queens, New York, where Jaydee was then training racehorses.

Jaydee and Marjorie resisted but Marguerite was steadfast; she showed up at the track day after day until she had convinced both Mooneys that they could trust her with their story. (Marguerite recalled she became so well accepted by the family she was even treated to a picnic lunch of Marjorie's fried chicken.)

In the meantime, Marguerite also managed to track down (with the help of Jackie George, the children's librarian at the Tulsa Public Library) trainer Hanley Webb's only living relative. George even accompanied Marguerite to the unnamed relative's home, where the relative reportedly told Marguerite she had no intention of talking—until Marguerite once more worked her charm. Marguerite asked polite questions about Hanley Webb's life and habits and avoided all discussions of horses. She assured the relative that she wanted to paint a complete picture of the man and her questions were correspondingly simple, straightforward: What did he look like? What did he eat? How did he live? She wisely skirted the more difficult matter of Black Gold's death.

As with her previous books, Marguerite was assisted by a phalanx of librarians, especially Jackie George and her fellow librarians from the Tulsa Public, along with her "regular" librarians, Roberta Sutton of the Chicago Public Library and the staff of the Elgin, Illinois, library. The Oklahoma librarians worked assiduously on Marguerite's behalf—she was a celebrity by then, after all. They compiled lists of Tulsa and Skiatook residents—anyone who may have known or remembered Rosa and Al Hoots and their ranch.

On-the-Road Research

Marguerite traveled to Oklahoma several times, visiting the places that would lend telling detail to her story. She visited the Hoots ranch (now called Black Gold Ranch) and house in Skiatook and even the nearby cottonwood tree where Marguerite imagined a blue jay that *"whistled G'night! G'night"* to Al and Rosa Hoots in the years before Black Gold was born, when they were both still dreaming of owning a great racehorse—before oil was discovered on the ranch, the great gushing so-called "black gold" that made the Hoots family fortune and gave a name to their horse.

The true story of Rosa and Al Hoots also unfolded during one of the darkest times in America's past—the killings of Osage Indians during the infamous "Reign of Terror" in the 1920s that saw an epidemic of murders and mysterious deaths among Osage tribe members who held "head rights" to oil fields. As with the terrible and sad elements of the "real" Brighty of the Grand Canyon story, this tragic history did not appear in Marguerite's book. Perhaps it was a history she did not know nor was told about when she arrived in Skiatook, some decades after Rosa (who was Osage) and Al Hoots were dead.

Marguerite traveled to Skiatook three times to take photographs to ensure she got the setting right. One such visit even made the local Skiatook paper. On March 14, 1957, a short piece stated: *"Visitors to*

Skiatook on Tuesday were Mrs. Jane Evelyn George, of the Tulsa Public Library, and Marguerite Henry, of Illinois. They were seeking information about the origin of the name 'Skiatook' and other interesting information concerning this community." The article notes that the two women were presented with a copy of a book about the history of Skiatook and "*referred to Scott Bradshaw and other longtime residents of Skiatook.*" Their interest in Black Gold was also highlighted.

A famous children's book author on a fact-finding mission wasn't only news in Skiatook, but in Tulsa too. *Tulsa World* chronicled Marguerite's Skiatook trip with remarkable attention to detail: "*It was a rainy, muddy day when Marguerite Henry, Jackie George and a newly acquired Skiatook friend set out to explore the countryside. Newly plowed fields, brambles, and barb-wire fence proved no deterrent as they scrambled down to Hominy Falls and scouted the countryside.*"

The town of Skiatook some twenty miles north of Tulsa (now considered a suburb of that city) is a town of ranch houses and low-slung buildings. Known as "The Gateway to the Osage," the town features a large sign notifying visitors "*You are entering Osage Nation Reservation.*" Skiatook was a much smaller town at the time of Marguerite's visits, with a population of around two thousand residents—nearly a quarter of its size today. The creation of the Skiatook Lake in 1984 added to its appeal, although the town went through hard times and many of the downtown stores stand empty. (Black Gold is still a point of pride; at the Black Gold Boarding House Antiques store, a jockey astride a black horse is positioned in front and a sign announces that the store is "*Named after the famous racehorse that was trained right here in Osage County.*" Marguerite's book is also on display.)

Marguerite traveled to Kentucky to see the farm where Black Gold had been born and to Lousiana, where Mooney grew up and learned to ride. She journeyed to the Fair Grounds track in New Orleans where

Mooney met Black Gold—and where Black Gold later ran his last race. Although Marguerite told the stories of Black Gold and Mooney separately for more than half of her book, she eventually knitted their narratives together in just a few evocative lines. *"For nearly two years, Black Gold and the boy, Jaydee, had lived unaware of each other's existence. When at last they did meet, Jaydee was jogging along on an early morning workout. He felt good. It was the kind of day when he wanted to stand up in his stirrups and push up to the clouds."*

That was the year that Black Gold turned two; it was the beginning of his racing career.

Psalms Were Written for Him

After winning the fiftieth Kentucky Derby in 1924, Black Gold continued to race, unlike top racehorses today, who may be retired after one or two big races. Rosa Hoots had originally put him "out to stud" for breeding purposes, but she returned him to the track after the horse failed to produce more than one foal. (The foal was later killed by lightning—a bad omen, it was thought.) Black Gold's return to racing at the age of six was inglorious. He didn't win a single race, thanks to a quarter crack in his hoof. (These vertical cracks between the heel and toe can make movement painful for a horse.) By then Mooney was no longer riding Black Gold, and in fact, he told Rosa Hoots and Webb not to race the horse until he was sound.

Hoots and Webb ran the horse in New Orleans anyway (for reasons that have never been fully documented nor explained), and Black Gold devastatingly broke down—but miraculously finished the race on three legs.

Black Gold's jockey that day was Dave Emery, whom Marguerite mentions only in passing at the end of the book. Emery, like Mooney, went on to train horses when he became too big to be a jockey. In an interview in *The Philadelphia Inquirer* on July 4, 1951, Emery described the fateful race: *"It looked like we'd win it. Then, at the furlong pole, Black Gold snapped his leg.... He was on three legs, you see!"* Emery recalled to sportswriter John Webster. Then Emery switched topics and went on to name a different horse—Prickly Heat—as the finest horse he'd ever ridden. *"He ran in distance races—just won and won."* (Perhaps Marguerite read this interview and decided that based on this rather heartless comment, Emery didn't deserve more than the barest mention in her book.)

The Chicago Tribune covered the news of Black Gold's death in a front-page 1928 story. Perhaps it was a story that Marguerite read or perhaps it was not, but surely, she knew that it was understood in the racing world that Black Gold had been retired "a hopeless cripple" for two years due to the quarter crack in his hoof before Webb decided to race him anyway. Marguerite does not mention this, nor the fact that Rosa Hoots refused the Kentucky Derby winning check of over fifty-two thousand dollars and demanded that Churchill Downs stewards pay her in cash (according to Fred Glueckstein in *Of Men, Women and Horses*—2006).

Although the end of Black Gold's life was undeniably tragic, Marguerite fashioned an ending more poignant than heartbreaking for her book, quoting an unnamed bystander at Black Gold's memorial service, a woman holding a poinsettia and a cross: *"Perhaps animals don't have souls but maybe Black Gold was an exception. And just maybe the Psalms were written for him as well as for the likes of us."* Was this something the great Thoroughbred trainer Ben Jones, who had won the Kentucky Derby six times and whom Marguerite had befriended, told her, since he was actually present on the day that Black Gold was buried? Or were they, in fact, Marguerite's own words? She certainly believed that animals had souls. In any case, it was the perfect epitaph.

The Wesley Dennis illustrations of Black Gold are every bit as heartfelt as Marguerite's prose, perhaps because he too had become good friends with the Mooneys, and his sensitivity to their plight and to the horse is equally palpable. As to the "real story" of Black Gold, according to Jaydee's grandson John Mooney, a retired racetrack official, Marguerite got most of the important facts right, while as in previous books, she shielded her audience from a few much sadder truths. According to John Mooney, there was nothing but greed behind the decision to run Black Gold, injured as he was, and no need to do so as Black Gold had earned over one hundred and ten thousand dollars in his short life—the equivalent of over two million dollars today.

John Mooney's grandfather Jaydee stopped riding horses the year after Black Gold died and began training them in Canada instead, which he did until he died of a heart attack in 1966 while on a hunting trip with his son. Mooney's grandmother Marjorie had been very involved in his grandfather's training operation, but Mooney said his grandparents were hesitant to talk about the tragedy of Black Gold. "My grandmother was reluctant to tell the story—she didn't like Webb," said Mooney. His grandmother's quibble with Marguerite's book was chiefly that she thought Marguerite's portrait of Hanley Webb made him seem better than he was in real life. Mooney also recalled that his grandmother told Rosa Hoots not to race Black Gold while he was lame, and Hoots would not listen.

Once again Marguerite gracefully trod a delicate line between the truth and the story she felt the world needed (and wanted) to hear; once more she struck the right balance between fiction and truth. The reviews of Black Gold were overwhelmingly positive. In The New York Times Book Review (1957), Ellen Lewis Buell noted that Marguerite "shuttles neatly from person to person, scene to scene to spin a narrative of triumph mixed with tragedy—but it is the tragedy that accents the *triumph."* Although Ms. Buell called Marguerite *"frequently, unabashedly sentimental"* in her writing, she acknowledged this was not something horse lovers often object to, especially when Marguerite *"can create such a sharp sense of immediacy as she does here."*

The reviewer of *The Children's Digest* (April 1958) was more generous in her assessment of the book: *"This racetrack story, involving a couple of men, a boy and two wonderful racehorses, is one of the best horse stories I have ever read."* Other reviewers offered similar words of praise (*"It has all the earmarks of a hit"*) and credited the *"very successful team"* of Marguerite and Dennis. Indeed, Dennis's work is noted in reviews just as often as Marguerite's for producing a book of warmth and heart. *"His pictures are terrific—so alive and spirited that you'd like to frame each one to enjoy every day,"* wrote Alberita Semrad in *The Chicago Tribune.* Meanwhile *The Virginian-Pilot* of Norfolk, Virginia (November 17, 1957) was not only admiring of the book but even bestowed a new title upon Marguerite. She was a "Horse Cultist" according to the reviewer: *"The real master of the horse story for this age is Marguerite Henry. With the breathless devotion of the true Horse Cultist, she tells the story of a Derby winner in Black Gold with expert illustrations by Wesley Dennis."*

As the critical kudos for *Black Gold* rolled out in newspapers across the country, Marguerite went on an extended book-signing tour, including a stop in Tulsa, Oklahoma, where she'd spent so much research time. The reviews of the event were (once again) as flattering to Marguerite herself as her book. *"When Marguerite Henry, one of America's most popular writers for boys and girls, wanted inspiration for her latest (and greatest) book she came to Oklahoma. Her personal charm and gracious nature opened doors that only years of research could have unlocked."*

A few years after *Black Gold's* publication, the Oklahoma Library Association presented Marguerite with the Sequoyah Children's Book

Award at a luncheon and "autograph party" in Ada, Oklahoma, in 1960. Fittingly the book had been chosen by Oklahoma school children, thirteen thousand of whom voted to give *Black Gold* the award. (The year before the children had voted to bestow the honors on the classic *Old Yeller* by Fred Gipson.) The event was covered in various Oklahoma papers; the reporter from the *Healdton Herald* (April 14, 1960) had an interesting take on the choice of books, pointing out the recent choices for the award were *"proof that children, in Oklahoma at least, are not deterred by sad endings."*

Misty Returns to Chincoteague

Although Marguerite had agreed with Grandpa Beebe that Misty should return to Chincoteague when Marguerite finished writing her book, she put off the pony's return year after year after year—until an entire decade had passed since Misty first arrived in Wayne as a tiny, shivering, decidedly woebegone foal.

But Marguerite realized that she couldn't—and shouldn't—delay Misty's departure forever. As she admitted in *A Pictorial Life Story of Misty*: *"I wore blinders to my selfishness and rationalized the delay. 'Let her have a happy colthood. Let her grow to her full strength...somehow, she belonged to our meadow... like a tree that has taken root."* She not only rationalized keeping Misty but by doing so, she ensured endless interest in the story of Misty and the book. Misty was a pet and a family member but also a brilliant marketing device.

There was her promise to Grandpa Beebe and the fact Marguerite knew that Misty ultimately belonged somewhere and with someone else (even if Misty technically belonged to her, thanks to Rand McNally). Marguerite wrote that the realization truly took hold one morning in June when she and Sid left Misty, Friday, and Jiggs in the care of a friend to attend a wedding in Wisconsin. The minister read a passage from the Book of Ecclesiastes at the wedding: *"To everything there is a season/and a time to every purpose/A time to be born and a time to die/A time to weep and a time to laugh..."* Marguerite took the words as a sign.

It was actually Sid who first broached the idea of Misty's return to Chincoteague. Perhaps it was finally time for Misty to go home, to have a foal of her own, to lead the life of a mother, Sid had suggested. Perhaps it was time for Misty to have a new beginning, even if it did mark, for fifty-six-year-old Marguerite, a painful end. *"Maybe the end of a thing could be better than the beginning,"* Marguerite wrote *A Pictorial Life Story of Misty.* *"Maybe life was just beginning for Misty."*

Marguerite's pain may have been somewhat assuaged by the many celebrations that followed and the considerable media coverage of Misty's departure from Wayne. Grandpa Beebe commissioned a friend from Chincoteague to pick Misty up in a truck that sported a very large and very specific sign: MISTY OF CHINCOTEAGUE GOES HOME TO HAVE HER COLT complete with a picture of Marguerite's book. Grandpa Beebe was clearly no slouch when it came to publicity.

The sign-emblazoned truck rolled past a Wayne church on Sunday morning as the parishioners were walking out the door, and according to Marguerite, they raised a collective cry of dismay and quickly descended upon Marguerite's yard. It was such a calamitous-seeming event that the Wayne School was closed the following day to mark Misty's departure, just as they had every year to celebrate Misty's birthday.

"We all thought we were going to die when she sent Misty back," recalled Ed Richardson. Before the festivities began, Drexler and Richardson took one last ride with Marguerite: Drexler on Jiggs, Richardson on Misty, and Marguerite on Friday. The trio sang "Onward

Christian Soldiers" together as they walked and trotted along, although the words were delivered in decidedly subdued tones.

Marguerite had alerted the papers to Misty's impending move back east, and quite a few, including *The Chicago Tribune,* covered the emotional leave-taking in full celebrity fashion. As the pony paparazzi showed up with cameras and notebooks, school children swarmed, many carrying homemade "Goodbye Misty" signs. Boys and girls crowded around for a last touch of the famous pony, who was wearing a horseshoe wreath made of carrots, or a picture of themselves with their favorite pony. Some particularly devoted fans even chased after the truck when it eventually pulled away and out to the Army Trail Road.

Around the same time as Misty's return to Chincoteague in April 1957, Paul Beebe, just twenty-one years old, was tragically killed in a car accident not far from the Beebe ranch. A local paper reported that the car went off the road and crashed into the home of George Ross with such force it pushed the house off its foundation. Just two months later, the Beebe family tragedy was compounded when Clarence "Grandpa" Beebe passed away in a Maryland hospital, although according to a letter from Ida ("Grandma") Beebe to Marguerite entitled "My dear Mrs. Henry," he had been able to ride Misty in public (sometime in May) soon after the pony's return to the island. *"Clarence rode her in the parade on Armed Forces Day and won a beautiful gold cup for being the prettiest pony in the parade,"* she wrote.

In the same letter Ida Beebe notified Marguerite that she would be selling books at the upcoming carnival where she would share their percentage with *"the Firemans."* Beebe ordered four hundred *Misty* books and one hundred *Sea Star* books and one hundred of *"the little book Misty the Island Pony that sell for 25 cents."* (With the latter it seems Grandma Beebe may have meant *Misty the Wonder Pony,* a Rand

McNally Elf Book—which were a series of small illustrated hardbacks for young readers priced at twenty-five cents). Beebe also requested that Marguerite mail five hundred stickers that she might put into the books. *"If there is a charge for so many please send me the bill,"* Beebe wrote, extending an invitation to Marguerite to visit Misty anytime.

Many years after Misty and both Grandpa and Grandma Beebe had passed away, Jeanette Beebe, Paul's aunt, seventy-one years old and working as a cook in the local school at the time, observed to a local reporter of *The Daily Press* of Newport News, Virginia, that a lot of things that happened to the Beebe family *"were not suitable for children's books"* (July 26, 1989). She cited hardships that included not only the death of Paul but also her son and her husband Ralph in 1969. Compounding the feeling of loss was the fact that much of the original Beebe Ranch was sold over the years; the ranch that Marguerite described in the pages of her book no longer existed.

In *A Pictorial Life Story of Misty*, Marguerite wrote about the collective hopes for Misty's foal. There is no mention of Paul's tragic death, although Marguerite wrote at length about his grandfather's passing, and surely she must have been terribly distraught by the loss of the two Beebes—a family she had spent so much time with—so abruptly and so close together. She and Wesley Dennis chartered a private plane to attend Grandpa's memorial service. There was a life-size model of Misty at the service, and afterward, Marguerite visited Misty at the Beebe Ranch, accompanied by Maureen.

Her time with Maureen wasn't without incident. Marguerite wrote that she was outraged to find Misty standing in a small dark shed with no straw on the floor, and how distressing it was to find that Misty looked thinner—and sadder as well. Marguerite was angry about Misty's condition, but Maureen assured her that Misty was stalled in the dark on account of the terrible mosquitos that plagued the island.

That was all that Marguerite wrote about her visit to Misty, save for the moment when she and Dennis took off in their small plane, leaving Chincoteague behind. Her observation at the time seems at odds with her earlier distress: *"Wesley and I were quiet in the realization how completely the Beebes had become our family too."*

It took a few years for Misty to have her first foal—in fact, it wasn't until the same year that Marguerite's next book (*Gaudenzia: Pride of the Palio*) was published that Misty's first foal was born (she would ultimately have three), when Misty was an "older" pony at fourteen years old. It was a momentous occasion for all, including Marguerite, who flew down in March 1960 in hopes of seeing the birth, but she had to leave for Washington DC before the foal—who Marguerite wanted to name Little Wisp—was born the following month.

Helen J. Perry of the *News Journal* (Delaware) covered Marguerite's trip to the island, with careful attention paid to Marguerite's appearance. She was a *"young looking woman in her 40s"* wrote Perry (Marguerite was actually fifty-eight years old) who came attired in a fur coat, tailored suit, and *"a close fitting hat."* Perry's next few lines weren't quite as flattering. Instead of highlighting Marguerite's Newbery Award and status as a bestselling author, Perry described Marguerite as the wife of an owner of several variety stores in Illinois (Sid still owned several Ben Franklin stores) and a *"housewife"* from Illinois. This must have surely vexed Marguerite as she made sure to tell Perry that her next book, *Gaudenzia: Pride of the Palio,* would be published later that year, and it was one for which she'd had to travel to Italy three times to research. The hapless Perry, meanwhile, not only shaved over ten years off Marguerite's age and called Marguerite a "housewife," but committed perhaps an even more egregious error when she referred to Misty having parties "on his birthday."

letters

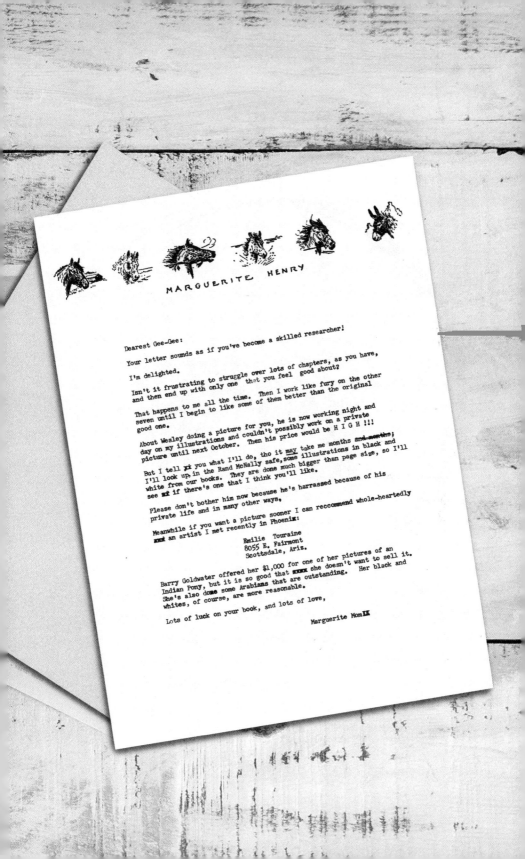

MARGUERITE HENRY

Dearest Gee-Gee:

Your letter sounds as if you've become a skilled researcher!

I'm delighted.

Isn't it frustrating to struggle over lots of chapters, as you have,
and then end up with only one that you feel good about?

That happens to me all the time. Then I work like fury on the other
seven until I begin to like some of them better than the original
good one.

About Wesley doing a picture for you, he is now working night and
day on my illustrations and couldn't possibly work on a private
picture until next October. Then his price would be H I G H !!!

But I tell you what I'll do, tho it may take me months and months;
I'll look up, in the Rand McNally safe, some illustrations in black and
white from our books. They are done much bigger than page size, so I'll
see if there's one that I think you'll like.

Please don't bother him now because he's harrassed because of his
private life and in many other ways,

Meanwhile if you want a picture sooner I can reccommend whole-heartedly
an artist I met recently in Phoenix:

                    Emilie Touraine
                    8055 E. Fairmont
                    Scottsdale, Ariz.

Barry Goldwater offered her $1,000 for one of her pictures of an
Indian Pony, but it is so good that she doesn't want to sell it. Her black and
She's also done some Arabians that are outstanding.
whites, of course, are more reasonable.

Lots of luck on your book, and lots of love,

                              Marguerite Mom II

10

GAUDENZIA,
PRIDE OF THE PALIO

CHAPTER TEN

"The mare pricked her ears. Whatever it was the boy
had said made a nice melody. She raised her head and let out
a whinny that bounced back and forth from the stone walls
again and again until it faded in a trembly echo.
'I bear you no ill will,' it said more plainly than any words."

—

FROM *Gaudenzia, Pride of the Palio*
(First Published 1960)

It was yet another librarian, the redoubtable Della McGregor, who planted the seed for Marguerite's next book. McGregor had been reading about the Palio di Siena—a brutal, dangerous horse race that takes place each year in Italy—and she passed the story along to Marguerite. Perhaps it was worthy of a book? Marguerite was immediately enthusiastic and began reading as much as she could about the historic race.

The timing was propitious; with Misty back in Chincoteague and the excitement over her departure in the past, Marguerite needed a new idea, a new goal, a fresh distraction, especially in the form of book that required a long research trip. Marguerite and her editor Mary Alice Jones spent hours at Marguerite's house considering possible ways that Marguerite might tell the story of the Palio, and the difficulties of reporting it too, not the least of which was the fact that Marguerite spoke no Italian at all.

The language gap did not deter Marguerite nor did the fact that she would need to travel to Siena, Italy, to "report" the book (a decidedly ambitious undertaking in the late 1950s)—the latter was actually hugely appealing to Marguerite, who immediately began saving money for the trip.

Marguerite wasn't so much interested in the race itself but was looking instead for a personal story to tell. She needed to find a noble horse with a brave young rider (preferably real) who took part in the Palio—an event she viewed as less of a race than a battle. But could she find one?

According to Marguerite's later account of what would eventually be three trips to Italy, she filled in conversational gaps with the natives with hand gestures that seemed sufficiently "Italian" to her when confronted by non-English speakers. (One can only imagine how these gestures were received by the residents—although Marguerite reported there was much laughter all around at her attempts to communicate.) Happily, she made the acquaintance of a local Siena barber who had studied English in school and could serve as her translator when he wasn't cutting hair. The barber, a young man named Giuseppe Bosi (noted as her guide in Siena in the credits section of the book), served as Marguerite's interpreter for much of her in-person research. On the days that Giuseppe Bosi had to cut hair, Marguerite ventured out on her own. *"These interviews proved hilarious,"* she noted, although sadly without sharing any of the "hilarious" details.

With the linguistic assistance of her barber-interpreter, Marguerite talked with Siena townspeople, professors, and horsemen. She spoke with the official starter of the Palio race, as well as Siena's chief magistrate, and she sent a letter to His Eminence Pope John XXIII, whom she later described as *"darling."* (*Gaudenzia's* hero Giorgio is invited to visit the Vatican after winning the Palio, so perhaps Marguerite asked the Pope a few questions about what the Vatican might have looked like inside.) Marguerite didn't furnish details as to what her contacts provided. She only offered this neat summing-up: *"Each one gave me a piece of the story until everything fitted neatly in place."* She makes it sound like such a simple proposition, except, of course, Marguerite wrote multiple drafts of every book. Fitting together the puzzle pieces actually took a great deal of work.

Gaudenzia is the story of Giorgio (who does not speak a word of English) and a beautiful gray half-Arabian mare named Gaudenzia. Both were "real" and still living when Marguerite arrived in Siena and decided they should be the stars of her book. The plot roughly follows the true facts of Giorgio's early career as a *contrada* rider (a *contrada* is a city ward or district, and race riders represent them in the Palio) and of Gaudenzia's life. Marguerite describes the danger of a race held on city streets, the ruthlessness of the race riders, and the bravery of the horses in vivid detail. In the Palio, the horse wins, whether he has a rider on his back or not.

A New Artist

Wesley Dennis chose not to illustrate *Gaudenzia* (it was said that he disapproved of the brutal nature of the Palio races) so Marguerite had to find another artist of equal talent and stature. Lynd Ward was a highly regarded children's book illustrator, easily the professional equal of Dennis—he had recently won the Caldecott Medal for *The Biggest Bear,* which he had both written and illustrated. (The book tells the story of a boy who befriends a bear cub and persuades men not to shoot him. Instead, they capture the bear and put him in a zoo where the boy can visit him "whenever he wants"—a happy ending for the boy, but perhaps not the bear.)

Ward was particularly famous for wood engravings and his so-called "wordless novels" (which are said to have paved the way for contemporary graphic novels). In terms of reputation, he seemed like a good fit for the book, and it was a plus that he too was from the Midwest—Chicago, in fact. Ward's father had been a minister in Chicago who later moved his family to New Jersey, where Ward's first-grade art teacher commended his work and possibly set the stage for his career when she told him that his last name was "draw" spelled backward. After high school graduation, Ward attended Columbia University in New York, where he met and married May McNeer, a highly accomplished author of children's books in her own right and later his partner on several books too.

When Marguerite met the Wards, they were living in Cresskill, New Jersey—an affluent town close to the George Washington Bridge—and New York City. Their house was located on a lovely private road named Lambs Lane built by the wealthy Lamb family, whose residence was located there as well. (The road was the source of the title for a children's book that the Wards jointly produced: *The Wolf of Lamb's Lane*—a story of three little girls and an eccentric neighbor woman who could cast spells.)

Marguerite described her meeting with the Wards as a *"fast moving afternoon and evening"* as the three discussed her idea for *Gaudenzia* and relived their experiences of traveling in Italy. Ward agreed to illustrate the book that Marguerite described as *"fiction-based-on-fact story of the historic race."* Ward's style was strikingly different from Wesley Dennis's, as was his approach to illustration—unlike Dennis, who liked nothing more than to sketch in a field surrounded by animals, Ward never worked from real life, according to Marguerite. *"Aside from rough sketching in the field he has never worked from a live model,"* she said.

Ward's partnership with Marguerite was very different from her partnership with Dennis in other regards. While she and Dennis has been equal partners in every book that they jointly produced—with Dennis's illustrations reflecting the emotion in Marguerite's words—Ward worked largely on his own, without constant contact with Marguerite. Could this be why the horses depicted in *Gaudenzia* seem to lack much expression? Was it Ward's lack of connection to the actual animal, the real Gaudenzia, who was then still living in Siena, or the lack of back and forth with Marguerite? Whatever the reason(s), the book is markedly different in artistic terms.

The book was also an enormous cultural reach for Marguerite, who spent time with Giorgio and his family in the Maremma region, which was then a rural, rather backward and poor coastal region in Tuscany. (Today, Maremma is home to some of the greatest wines produced in Tuscany and vacation homes of wealthy and aristocratic families.) Since no one in Giorgio's family, including Giorgio, spoke English, Marguerite often resorted to many of the same "pantomime" gestures that she'd employed during her time in Siena.

Perhaps the fact that Marguerite did not speak the language was why some critics noted the often-stilted nature of the book's dialogue, which can read, at times, like an imperfect translation. For example, this conversation between Giorgio and the Chief-of-the-Guards about Gaudenzia the horse: *"With her what would I do? Where would I keep her?"* the Chief asked. A few lines later, Giorgio's reply. *"In the Maremma I can winter her. Babbo has a very nice barn. Nobody lives there. Nobody but Pippa our donkey."*

"Read...and Let Your Dreams Run Away"

Marguerite glossed over some, but not all, the unpleasant facts about Giorgio's life, including the fact that his father raised horses to sell for slaughter. On the other hand, Marguerite wrote accurately of what poverty in rural Italy in the 1950s was like, in an era when few Americans knew much about Italian culture or its food or people, and the country was still recovering from the effects of World War II. But the subject of the book may have been too obscure for American readers of the time, as the book reportedly did not sell as well as many of its predecessors. Was it the obscurity of the race or its brutality or the then-limited interest in Italian culture? Whatever the reasons, the book would later be reissued with a new title: *The Wildest Horse Race in the World.*

The Walt Disney Company expressed interest in a possible movie about Gaudenzia and the Palio, and a production team even traveled to Italy to film scenes, but as Marguerite explained to a young reader named Maria many years later, there were too many obstacles to overcome for the film to be made, including the fact that the people of Siena did not want any other horse but Gaudenzia—by then too old to race—to appear in the film. The people of Siena also refused to rerun the race, Marguerite noted in "The Story Behind the Story of Gaudenzia" in her newsletter. *"Again, I felt defeated,"* Marguerite wrote. *"Until a remark by Wesley comforted me. 'The best pictures,' he said, 'are always taken in your own mind anyway.' So dear friends, read and let your dreams run away."*

As one who regularly allowed her dreams to guide her, Marguerite could very well have been writing the note to herself.

letters

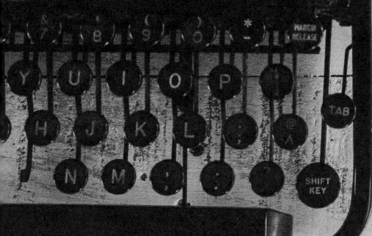

June 18, 1984

Dear Margeruite

I'm writing a book with each chapter being a story and I was wondering if you woud please help me publish it and help me with writing it. I've got plans to write each story about a horse named Vanilla who is a palimino with a bit of dapple on her stomach. (She's the one I ride at Horseman's park.) Also could you ask Wesley Dennis to do ~~all~~ Illustrations for me? Tell him he can draw a picture with his choice except I was wanting the horse to be in every picture! Well I've got to go do my evening chores, but if you ever came around Scripps Ranch be sure to stop by and go swimming and tell me any ideas you have for books.

Your #1 fan.

Jenifer Reins

Jenifer Lynn Reins,
10719 Charbono Ter.,
San Diego, CA. 92131.

11

STORMY, MISTY'S FOAL

11

"Paul and Maureen stood on tiptoe, peering in without breathing.
They were utterly still, not wanting the scene to change.
There, at the far end of the stall, stood Misty.
She eyed them dispassionately, as if they belonged to another world
and another time. Like a bird brooding a chick,
she was hovering over a wise little, fuzzy little, scraggly little foal."

—

FROM *STORMY, MISTY'S FOAL*
(FIRST PUBLISHED 1963)

P*onies may have been wiped out,* declared the headline of a front-page story in the *Daily Times* of Salisbury, Maryland, after a devastating storm struck the Virginia shoreline, including Assateague and Chincoteague Islands, on the first week of March in 1962. Many of the wild ponies on Assateague were killed, homes on Chincoteague were destroyed, and thousands of residents were evacuated. Misty was about to give birth. And Marguerite was in Austria researching her next book.

It was also less than nine months after the 20th Century Fox movie *Misty* had premiered on the island. Ralph Beebe, son of Grandpa and Grandma Beebe and uncle to Paul and Maureen, was at the Beebe Ranch, looking after Misty and the other ponies, and in the beginning, it seemed as though they might be spared. But by the early hours of the morning, a high tide hit Chincoteague and water began to enter Misty's barn. Beebe decided to bring Misty, pregnant with her third foal, into his house, where she remained in the kitchen for three days, until the tides had receded enough that Beebe could drive her to a veterinary office in Maryland. Misty gave birth to her foal Stormy on Sunday, March 11, at Dr. Finney's in Pocomoke, Maryland. The local paper reverentially described Dr. Finney as having *officiated at the expected blessed event.*

It was estimated that the storm caused over thirty million dollars in damage to Chincoteague (about two hundred and fifty million in today's dollars) and raised grave concerns that typhoid might strike the island. President John F. Kennedy declared Chincoteague a federal disaster area and dispatched civil defense workers who set up typhoid inoculation stations for residents and rescue workers. The Army and National Guard moved in to clear away mountains of debris from the destroyed businesses and homes—and the dead animals. A helicopter tour of Assateague Island revealed that at least seventy-five of the wild ponies had survived the high water and winds, although even more—including pregnant mares and foals—had drowned. The loss was no less than utterly devastating.

The press made much of the fact that Misty had weathered the storm stalled in the kitchen of Ralph Beebe's home. (A bit less attention was paid to Ralph Beebe himself, though he was interviewed endlessly about Misty's well-being during those critical three days that she was living in his house.) For his part, Beebe was quick to credit Misty for her tidiness, which was doubtless thanks to the many years she'd spent walking around inside Sid and Marguerite's home in Wayne. Misty had left his family's kitchen in remarkably good shape, Ralph reported, and even enjoyed a few privileges. *"The only thing I did was let her drink out of the kitchen sink, which my wife would not approve of if she knew it,"* said Ralph, who cleaned up the kitchen afterward.

Although, as previously noted, Marguerite had pledged not to write a "Misty Part Two," she'd written *Sea Star* more than ten years before the storm (1949), and now clearly Mother Nature had delivered her another remarkable true-life sequel. There was no question that there would be a book about the series of events.

It took Marguerite a few days to get a plane ticket home from Vienna, where she was researching the book that would become *White Stallion of Lipizza*. (In a recorded 1968 "Meet the Authors" interview produced by Imperial International Learning, she said she learned of the storm from a newspaper while in Vienna.) Marguerite later rather dramatically recounted her feelings at being so far away at such a critical time: *"I had to get out of Vienna! I had to get to Chincoteague! Misty was in danger! She might need me! How could I be thousands of miles away when Misty was going to have a baby! Already I felt like its grandmother!"* (That last line appears in the book *Stormy, Misty's Foal*, spoken by Maureen when she first views Misty and her baby.)

By the time Marguerite arrived in Chincoteague—stylishly attired in a fur coat and hat (duly noted by the press)—Misty had delivered her foal and Dr. Finney's eight-year-old son David (who looked much like a young Paul Beebe) had been much-photographed, sitting on Misty and holding Stormy in the pictures that accompanied news of Stormy's birth. When Marguerite's editor Mary Alice Jones saw the photographs in *Life* magazine, she wrote to Marguerite: *"The little boy looks like a charming prospect for a new human hero. And the frisky foal is a heartwarming bit of the animal kingdom!"* Jones offered further encouragement: *"I know that before too long another book laid in Chincoteague will come to delight the children, please the librarians and rejoice the heart of the publisher—not to mention give pleasure to the author who creates it!"*

Mauled by the Sea

The story that Marguerite would tell in *Stormy, Misty's Foal* included the devastation of the island that Marguerite witnessed firsthand, and she didn't spare the distressing details. *"It was a horrible heartbreaking sight, mauled by the sea!"* Marguerite wrote. And the fact that the storm hit at a time when Misty was due to foal was additional, actual drama that would end up in the book. *"Nothing had to be made up! Neither fear nor danger nor suspense!"* Of course, that wasn't exactly true. As with *Misty of Chincoteague*, the facts of *Stormy* were very much intermingled with fiction, as it was of course Ralph Beebe, not Paul nor Grandpa (both of whom were dead), who had kept Misty safe in the storm.

Marguerite imagined how Grandpa Beebe might comfort Maureen and Paul as the storm raged. *"'There, there children, hold on,' Grandpa soothed. 'Buckle on your blinders and let's think of Fun Day.'"* she wrote. Marguerite willed Grandpa Beebe and Paul back to life, and Grandma too, in the role of looking after Misty and putting her in the kitchen of their house. *"'I'll stay with Misty,' Grandma announced without turning around. 'Much as I dislikes treating ponies like folks, I can admit to a kinship when she's having a baby.'"* The touching illustrations by Wesley Dennis of Maureen riding Misty up the stairs of the house in the storm with Grandpa waiting to receive them showed the family alive and well and exactly where Marguerite, and her readers, wanted them to be (still).

Marguerite returned to the facts of what actually happened, when in the book Misty is driven to Dr. Finney's in Pocomoke, Maryland, to deliver her foal.

When it was time to name Misty's new baby, schoolchildren from across the country actually did write hundreds of letters with suggestions of names. Although they arrived addressed to Grandpa and Grandma Beebe and Maureen and Paul in the book, they were letters that Ralph Beebe received in real life, and they included this one: *"If I owned Misty, I would name her colt 'Stormy.'"* Ralph and Marguerite jointly chose the name Stormy.

How was Marguerite able to retell a story that so clearly collided with recent history? After all, the deaths of both Paul and Grandpa Beebe had been reported in local newspapers. But the fact that they were long dead when *Stormy, Misty's Foal* takes place seems to have passed unmentioned not only by the press but even Chincoteaguers themselves. Was it that Marguerite simply did not want to let go of the characters whom her readers had grown to love? Or did she want to pretend their lives, and her life, hadn't changed since the time she first met them so long ago, when Paul and Grandpa were still alive, and Misty, Maureen, Marguerite, and Wesley Dennis were still (fairly) young? Everyone in Chincoteague, it seemed, (also) wished that it was so.

Of course, Marguerite, as always, did a great deal of research about the storm and its aftermath, and the facts are meticulously noted as she adroitly balanced what was real with what she imagined had transpired. She composed a long list of questions for Ralph as to exactly what happened to Misty during the storm, and his answers became Paul's words in the book. *"What about drinking water? How did you feed her? Was Stormy born on a Sunday? Where did the birth take place?"* Marguerite queried. Enough of the details were so well researched that her publishers boldly asserted: *"Like all Marguerite Henry stories, it is based upon actual fact,"* on the book's flap copy. Or as Marguerite said at a banquet held in her honor at a school book fair, her books were "90 percent fact and 10 percent little bridges" (*The Pantagraph,* November 22, 1964, Bloomington, Illinois).

The reviews of *Stormy* were uniformly positive (*"The author capably has balanced extremes of grief and courage and joy, while keeping her story entirely real,"* wrote reviewer Jane Thomas for the *Star Tribune of Minneapolis*) and advertisements echoed Marguerite's assertion that the story of Stormy was real (*"based on actual fact"* and *"the true and thrill-packed story"*). The same newspapers that reported that Ralph Beebe was the owner of Stormy also reported that the story of Stormy was real. The actual *actual* facts failed to affect the book's popularity or dim its appeal.

Book sales were bolstered by occasional in-person appearances of real-life Misty and real-life Stormy while Marguerite and Wesley Dennis once again participated in book signings all over the country. *Stormy, Misty's Foal* was truly a resounding success: number three on the *"New York Times* Best Sellers" children's books list in November 1964, besting such legendary books as Dr. Seuss's *The Cat in the Hat* and Maurice Sendak's *Where the Wild Things Are*. (The number one book that year was *Mary Poppins* by P.L. Travers.)

letters

Wayne, Illinois
Tel. 584 3994

Donnerstag morgen
30. 4. 1964

Colonel Alois Podhajsky

Dear Colonel Podhajsky:

I am sorry to say that the large oil painting which I had
hoped to show you after the performance tonight is already
at the lithographers being reproduced for the "jacket" of
the book.

Perhaps this is just as well, for with the great crowd of
people so eager to talk with you, the painting might become
damaged.

It was painted by the same artist, Wesley Dennis, who
illustrated the Lipizzan chapter in the Album of Horses
which you liked so well. This new painting is, I believe,
one of his most magnificent.

My part of the story goes to the printer the first of July,
and the book will be published in November.   Fortunately
it will be priced low enough so that many families can afford
it for their children. For it is these very children who
have been writing me for more, more, more about the Lipizzaners.

It was good to learn from you last night that Borina lived out
his days in his own stall at the Reitschule. That is a perfec
ending to the book.

Please tell Mrs. Podhajsky that I enjoyed pinning the bunch
of violets on her gown. She is most beautiful, and gracious.

I have listed my telephone number above in the event that
you both might like an interlude of peace and quiet in
suburban Chicago "auf diem Land."

Sincerely,

12

WHITE STALLION
OF LIPIZZA

CHAPTER TWELVE

"In his mind he saw the great palace in Vienna
and the eight snow-white stallions doing the quadrille,
and he was one of the riders—not thinking
of the audience at all, only wanting to be trusted
and understood by the one creature he rode."

—

FROM *WHITE STALLION OF LIPIZZA*
(FIRST PUBLISHED 1964)

Where else can you find a horse stable with chandeliers?" asked Walt Oleksy in *The Chicago Tribune* (April 5, 1959) as he extolled the attractions of Vienna and the city's Spanish Riding School. Where else indeed? About the time that Mr. Oleksy posed his question, Marguerite had been thinking about Vienna herself. She was reading a book about the history of the school and the white Lipizzaner stallions saved from the Nazis by Colonel Alois Podhajsky, the Riding School's director. She was determined to visit Vienna and see its famed Spanish Riding School, but she also wanted to figure out a way to tell the story of the Colonel's act of bravery.

While Colonel Alois Podhajsky was a heroic figure and a master of classical dressage, his boyhood years were long since past—he was actually several years older than Marguerite. Furthermore, when Marguerite wrote the Colonel in 1960 about her desire to write a book centered on the school, the Colonel had been firmly discouraging. *"I think it will not be very successful to find a long true story,"* he replied, adding, *"The reason is, there are not many true stories and a lot of books with stories of the Lipizzan horses... So I really do not know what story you should write about these (sic) in the world so well-known horses."*

Marguerite, however, was far from discouraged. Four years following that initial correspondence, Marguerite had not only written about the Spanish Riding School in *White Stallion of Lipizza,* and turned out *Stormy, Misty's Foal* as well as a charming but very short book called *Five O'Clock Charlie* (illustrated by Wesley Dennis), she and Colonel Podhajsky had also become regular correspondents, perhaps even friends.

How had Marguerite managed to change the Colonel's mind? As Marguerite explained in an essay titled "The Four-Footed Professor" that she wrote the same year the book appeared, she sent first a "pleading" letter to Colonel Podhajsky, asking if there was a story of a young boy and a Lipizzaner stallion that she might use for a book, and having received the reply that seemed discouraging, Marguerite took a different tack. She decided to focus on the Colonel's words *"there are not many true stories."* She decided they meant *she* could be the one who would finally write a "true" book.

The undaunted Marguerite next wrote the Colonel that she was planning to visit, and that she and Sid had booked tickets to Austria—perhaps she and the Colonel could meet? Her determination was rewarded with an hour spent in the Colonel's company the day the

Henrys arrived in Vienna. The Colonel's office was *"so beautiful it seemed unreal,"* Marguerite later wrote in "The Four-Footed Professor." Filled with paintings and horse statues, the office—like the Colonel himself—was intimidating. But then Marguerite saw Colonel Podhajsky's dog, which was a dachshund, just like her pup Alex. *"I took courage. If a dog and horses like a man, I had nothing to worry about,"* she wrote. Once more, Marguerite had found a way in.

An Editor's Influence

The Colonel spent much of their time together reminiscing about Maestoso Borina, the great white stallion whom he called "The Four-Footed Professor," as the stallion knew a great deal more than his young riders and helped teach them what to do and how to ride. Marguerite liked the name so much she wanted to call the book she was writing "The Four-Footed Professor," and imagined it would be a small picture book like *Five O'Clock Charlie*, the book she had just written with Dennis about a draft horse in England who loved to eat tarts. But the more time Marguerite spent at the school observing the riders, the more convinced she became that she needed to write a much longer book—as did her editor, Mary Alice Jones.

It was truly Jones who made Marguerite think about the project in a much larger way, Marguerite later recounted. When she returned to Illinois and met with Jones, her editor peppered her with questions. *"Why are they called Lipizzaners? And why is it the Spanish Riding School?"* Jones wanted more of a story, and her questions goaded Marguerite into a search for the answers.

Marguerite had plenty of notes to draw upon from the time she'd spent sitting in the Colonel's viewing box at the arena in Vienna—watching riders, scribbling notes about their positions and the look of the horses. The men *"sat like stone in the saddles"* and *"the apprentices may start as pupils at 9 years and remain until 65,"* she wrote, with many scratched-out corrections to previous notes. She talked with the young apprentice riders at the school and even traveled to the Alps to see where Lipizzaners were bred. But she didn't find a hero to play the central role in her book.

So she decided to make one up.

Marguerite's hero, a baker's son named Hans Haupt who aspired to ride the great Lipizzaner horses, was a composite of the sort of boys whom Marguerite met while visiting the Spanish Riding School. She decided his story would be the sort of "Horatio Alger tale" that readers loved, and she loved to tell. Thus Hans Haupt, baker's boy, became the hero who fell in love with the dancing white horses, and specifically with the one great (real) horse Borina, who was the pride of Colonel Alois Podhajsky.

Attention to Accuracy

Although Hans was fictional, much of the book included the facts that Marguerite had gleaned about horsemanship and classical dressage from the Colonel, and she carefully fact-checked the details with him and with others—none were too small, although it seemed her diligence was occasionally ill-timed. In a letter to the Colonel, Marguerite extended her condolences for the loss of his wife, then got down to business with a series of detailed questions about the school and its riders: *"Do you yourself often interview these apprentices? Do you yourself go to the farm to select certain colts? How are the colts transported from The Piber to Vienna? Could I have a copy of the rules the rider must abide by?"* and on and on. (Leaving nothing to chance or misinterpretation, she sent the letter in German as well.)

Marguerite even sent a letter to a Viennese librarian named Mr. Hasse (June 11, 1964) with questions about library protocol. *"Is there a warning bell before the closing hour and then the final bell? Or how do you notify the patrons who may be slow in leaving?"* Marguerite asked. She had decided that Hans was a frequent visitor to the library, and so in the book it is the librarian, Fraulein Morgen, who gives him a ticket to see the "dancing horses" perform and to sit in the "Imperial Box" above the arena—the same box where Marguerite sat during her visit to Vienna. Hans, just like Marguerite, watches the stallion Borina perform "airs above the ground" (a series of higher-level classical dressage movements—jumps and kicks—where the horse's feet leave the ground) and imagines himself in the role of the rider. (The details in the writing are so accurate that a book critic even noted approvingly that Marguerite got all the "umlauts" right.)

White Stallion of Lipizza took longer than Marguerite had envisioned, as she had to cut her trip to Vienna short when she received word about Misty and the terrible Chincoteague storm. Her book about the Colonel and the Lipizzaner horses was then further delayed when her publisher, Rand McNally, wanted a story about Misty's foal and the island disaster to be published first.

The publicity around the publication of *Stormy, Misty's Foal* and the subsequent travel that was required for its promotion meant that *White Stallion of Lipizza* was delayed by yet another year. It wasn't until February 4, 1964, that Marguerite took up the research of the book again, but before the end of the year, the book was finally published, becoming another great success. The first printing of sixty thousand sold out in two weeks, a second printing of forty thousand was "almost consumed" by orders, and a third printing was scheduled. Marguerite and Wesley Dennis went on their customary book signing tour, appearing in book shops and department stores from Virginia to Cincinnati and

Dayton, Ohio, to Philadelphia with a stop in nearby Cherry Hill, New Jersey. The Camden, New Jersey, *Courier Post* covered their joint appearance at a Cherry Hill mall in a story by Jean V. Ross, published on November 21, 1964. (In the accompanying photograph, Marguerite is largely obscured by a large copy of *White Stallion of Lipizza* but wearing an exceedingly stylish leopard print hat. Dennis looked customarily rumpled in his suit and tie.) Ross described Marguerite as *"the tall blonde author."* (Interestingly, Marguerite was sometimes described as brown-haired and sometimes blonde, and once was even described as a redhead!) Marguerite was *"well known for her meticulous research and good story telling,"* according to Ross, who asked Marguerite how long it took her to write the book. Marguerite replied with her "eleven months line," likening herself to a mare in foal again, which she clearly liked to do. (When Marguerite came up with a good line, she was more than happy to use it over and over.)

The book received largely positive reviews leavened by a few tepid notes and more critical assessments. *The Pantagraph* (November 22, 1964) described *White Stallion of Lipizza* as *"factual and thus is a painless study of the Spanish Court of Riding School in Vienna."* And the reviewer for *The San Francisco Examiner* (August 1, 1965) was less impressed, finding the subject *"trite"* and labeling the book *"a popular-market piece."* The reviewer also seemed to take Marguerite to task for turning her books into movies. *"Miss Henry, now apparently solely beguiled by movie possibilities, has written a pleasant story about the Spanish Riding School horses."*

Colonel Podhajsky co-wrote the screenplay for the 1963 Disney movie *The Miracle of the White Stallions* and also published the English translation of his book *The White Stallions of Vienna,* detailing the history of the Spanish Riding School and the history of the Lipizzaner breed, in 1964. The appearance of the Colonel's book and the

Disney movie at about the same as Marguerite's book caused a bit of confusion, perhaps, in the mind of book reviewers like that of *The San Francisco Examiner*, who thought Marguerite's book was based on the movie or the Colonel's book, or both.

The Colonel retired in 1965, although he continued to teach dressage and inspire classical dressage riders around the world. As Marguerite wrote in her book, quoting Colonel Podhajsky: *"Our school is a small candle in a troubled world. If we can send out one beam of splendor, of glory, of elegance, it is worth a man's lifetime, no?"*

letters

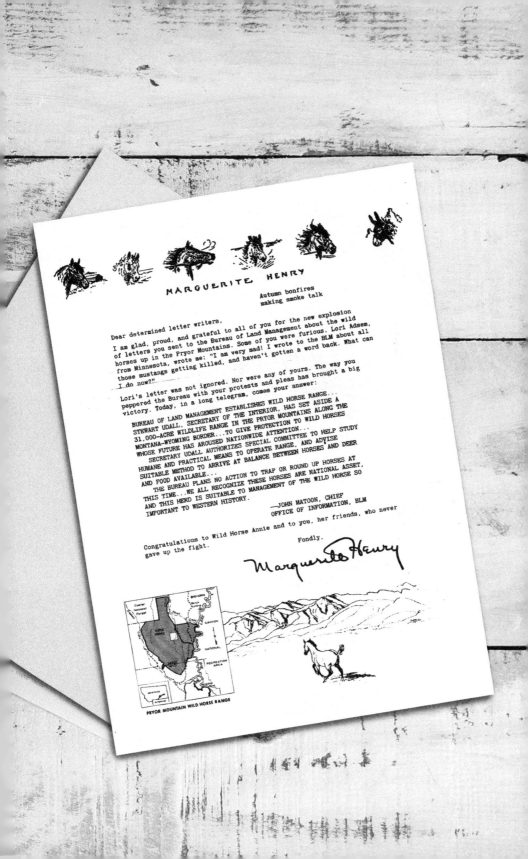

MARGUERITE HENRY

Autumn bonfires
making smoke talk

Dear determined letter writers,

I am glad, proud, and grateful to all of you for the new explosion
of letters you sent to the Bureau of Land Management about the wild
horses up in the Pryor Mountains. Some of you were furious. Lori Adsem,
from Minnesota, wrote me: "I am very mad! I wrote to the BLM about all
those mustangs getting killed, and haven't gotten a word back. What can
I do now?"

Lori's letter was not ignored. Nor were any of yours. The way you
peppered the Bureau with your protests and pleas has brought a big
victory. Today, in a long telegram, comes your answer:

BUREAU OF LAND MANAGEMENT ESTABLISHES WILD HORSE RANGE...
STEWART UDALL, SECRETARY OF THE INTERIOR, HAS SET ASIDE A
31,000-ACRE WILDLIFE RANGE IN THE PRYOR MOUNTAINS ALONG THE
MONTANA—WYOMING BORDER...TO GIVE PROTECTION TO WILD HORSES
WHOSE FUTURE HAS AROUSED NATIONWIDE ATTENTION...
    SECRETARY UDALL AUTHORIZES SPECIAL COMMITTEE TO HELP STUDY
HUMANE AND PRACTICAL MEANS TO OPERATE RANGE, AND ADVISE
SUITABLE METHOD TO ARRIVE AT BALANCE BETWEEN HORSES AND DEER
AND FOOD AVAILABLE...
    THE BUREAU PLANS NO ACTION TO TRAP OR ROUND UP HORSES AT
THIS TIME...WE ALL RECOGNIZE THESE HORSES ARE NATIONAL ASSET,
AND THIS HERD IS SUITABLE TO MANAGEMENT OF THE WILD HORSE SO
IMPORTANT TO WESTERN HISTORY.

                              —JOHN MATOON, CHIEF
                               OFFICE OF INFORMATION, BLM

Congratulations to Wild Horse Annie and to you, her friends, who never
gave up the fight.

                    Fondly,

                    Marguerite Henry

PRYOR MOUNTAIN WILD HORSE RANGE

13

FAREWELL, OLD FRIEND: THE DEATH OF WESLEY DENNIS AND MUSTANG: WILD SPIRIT OF THE WEST

13

W esley and I had agreed not to attend each other's funeral. *That way the first one to depart this earth would remain forever a living memory,* Marguerite wrote in *The Illustrated Marguerite Henry.* While Wesley Dennis's obituary noted his death at sixty-three without specifying the ailment, according to his granddaughter Devon Settle, who lives in Virginia not far from the (former) family farm, her grandfather died of cirrhosis.

If Marguerite knew this, she offered no public acknowledgment of the fact, although as Dennis had been a heavy smoker and drinker, it would not be surprising that the combination took an eventual toll. According to his obituary,

Dennis "died after a long illness" in a Falmouth, Massachusetts, hospital, although on the day of his death Dennis had been swimming in the ocean off Cape Cod. It was September 1966, just before Marguerite's book *Mustang: Wild Spirit of the West*—illustrated by Robert Lougheed—debuted.

Dennis's death received national attention; his obituary appeared in papers all over the country with one (very) long obituary published in the Richmond, Virginia, *Times-Dispatch*. Dennis's name was linked with Marguerite's multiple times—their partnership, their many books (most notably, of course, *Misty of Chincoteague*), and Marguerite's tribute was quoted: *"Wesley Dennis has possibly illustrated more books about horses than any other contemporary artist,"* although there was no word from his family. Dennis's attachment to Marguerite, and to her celebrity, continued (long) after his death.

Interestingly, Dennis was noted as leaving behind a wife and children, although he and his wife Dorothy had actually divorced in 1961—five years before his death. (Dorothy Dennis died two years after her husband in 1968 at fifty-nine years of age.)

Shortly after Dennis's death, Dorothy wrote a long letter to May Massee in response to a note from Massee. *"You are right—he was one of your best friends... he was always proud of 'Flip' and it gave him more lasting pleasure than anything he ever did. It was always in the back of his mind to try to do another similar book."*

The idea that *Flip*, which Dennis wrote and illustrated *before* he and Marguerite met, was the work he cared for the most is a surprising assertion. Was it true or was it Dorothy Dennis's conjecture—an attempt to counter the idea that Dennis was so utterly bound up with Marguerite? Had the fact that Marguerite figured so greatly in Dennis's obituary fueled a desire to let Massee know that his solo work with Massee as his editor was what had mattered the most?

Dorothy Dennis recalled the early years of her marriage when she and Dennis were living in Massee's house in New York for a time, before moving to the farm in Virginia, with these poignant lines: *"Certainly my years in your house in Montgomery were the happiest in my life and I have mentally turned the pages back to that chapter many, many times."* She closed with the hope that they might see one another that winter in New York. But May Massee died just a few months later, on Christmas Eve. She was eighty-five years old.

A Year of Loss

In addition to the death of her partner and friend Wesley Dennis, Marguerite had suffered another great loss earlier in that same year, or rather, she had suffered the loss on behalf of her beloved sister Gertrude, whose husband Russell Jupp passed away quite unexpectedly, early in 1966. Although Jupp was seventy-six years old, the shock and the suddenness of his death were so great that Marguerite and Sid brought Gertrude to their home in Wayne for an extended period. Marguerite tended to her older sister as vigilantly as Gertrude had cared for her when they were children. Marguerite referenced her debt to Gertrude and the care she took of Marguerite when she was a child. *"She practically raised me, tutored me, and has been my mentor and alter ego ever since I was a little girl. Now it was my turn to help her."* After a few months, Gertrude returned home to *"rebuild her life,"* Marguerite said. (Gertrude went on to work at the Milwaukee-Downer College for many years and later served as the president of its Alumnae Association Board and as a public relations officer. In recognition of her work, the college created the Gertrude Breithaupt Jupp Outstanding Service Award, which is given to an alumna or alumnus who has been of service to the school.)

When Marguerite acknowledged Wesley Dennis's death in her third newsletter, her words were straightforward and crisply matter-of-fact. *"I know that you and all his fans will be shocked to hear that he died on September 3. He would not want you to sorrow,"* she wrote. *"He would want me to tell you that he went swimming in the Atlantic Ocean on his last day. He lived every moment of his life to the fullest. He never wanted to be an old man and he never was."*

As in all her writing, Marguerite shared just enough of the truth to be accurate, though she was carefully non-specific, sparing her young fans from the full facts of his death. She wanted readers to picture him happily swimming in the ocean on his last day on earth, knowing it was the image he'd want them to have, and perhaps the one that Marguerite wanted to hold as well—a vigorous and playful man with a puckish sense of fun. Her only public expression of deeply felt sorrow came when Marguerite admitted in letters to readers and friends that she wasn't sure that she could go on without Dennis as her illustrator, partner, and co-conspirator. Marguerite had even considered that she might stop writing altogether, although she had her newest book, *Mustang: Wild Spirit of the West,* to promote.

A Different Sort of Star

While some of the stars of Marguerite's books were fictional composites and some were real people who were still alive when the books about them were published, Wild Horse Annie aka Velma Johnston, the heroine of *Mustang: Wild Spirit of the West,* was an altogether different sort of star. The relationship that developed between Johnston and Marguerite was much closer than the real-life heroes of her previous works, and more complicated. In many ways, *Mustang* was Marguerite's most complex book.

David Cruise and Alison Griffiths, the husband-and-wife journalist team, wrote in their book *Wild Horse Annie and the Last of the Mustangs* that Marguerite first discovered Velma Johnston and her work on behalf of wild horses in the book *American Wild Horses* by B.F. Beebe and James Johnson. Cruise and Griffiths devoted several chapters to the relationship between Marguerite and Johnston, and their take on that relationship is often less than flattering to Marguerite.

According to Cruise/Griffiths, the story began with a phone call from Marguerite after reading the Beebe book—something that Marguerite herself later described. (She was first intrigued by the fact it was written by someone named Beebe, thinking it was a relative of the Beebe family in Chincoteague.) Marguerite described her discovery to a reporter from *The Jackson Sun* of Tennessee in 1966. She and her editor Mary Alice Jones had been casting about for ideas for a new book while sitting in Marguerite's study in Wayne, and when Marguerite handed Jones the Beebe book, the editor was taken with the idea of a book about Wild Horse Annie too.

Marguerite recounted the moment that the two women spent looking out over her snow-covered Midwestern lawn (it was early spring), and Marguerite imagined *"sage and juniper and pine and horses being rounded up."* Within weeks of that moment, Marguerite was on her way to Reno to meet "Annie" (Johnston) and her mother "Ma Bronn." Marguerite later noted, with some disappointment, that Johnston didn't look quite as Marguerite had pictured. When Johnston met Marguerite's plane in Reno, the writer was surprised to find a slim, well-dressed woman who looked like a secretary (as Johnston was) and not a *"rugged Westerner."* Johnston wasn't powerfully built but *"slender to the point of fragility."*

The story of Johnston's fight to save the Mustangs had begun many years earlier, long before she and Marguerite first met. It was 1950 and Johnston had followed a truck filled with terrified Mustangs to a rendering plant, which filled her with horror—and the resolve to do something to stop them. Johnston's campaign to save the wild horses was a long, often dangerous battle with ranchers and cattlemen who threatened her life (and led Johnson to carry a gun), but she persevered, and her work eventually led to a law to protect wild horses and burros, signed by President Dwight D. Eisenhower in 1959.

The story of Johnston's life and her fight to save the wild horses unspooled over many long, late-night conversations between the two women. Marguerite spent a week with Johnston and her mother on the first of what would be many trips to Nevada. She met with Johnston's friends and her employer, and traveled to the Virginia City, Nevada, courthouse where Johnston had first taken a stand against the roundup and slaughter of wild horses.

Marguerite also visited the Double Lazy Heart Ranch where Johnston and her late husband Charlie had once lived, immersing herself as completely in the daily details of Johnston's life as she had that of the Beebes, the Mooneys, and the Gibsons, although unlike all the other heroes of Marguerite's books, Johnston was still living the hero's role, and in fact, her work wasn't done.

Johnston was an accomplished public speaker (and writer) in her own right, thanks to her years of work on behalf of the Mustangs, but she admitted to being awestruck by Marguerite and her fame. *"I'm constantly amazed at how beautifully you handle all your commitments and seem so unhurried and unruffled all the time. Do you have a secret formula?"* Johnston asked Marguerite in one of their many letters (from *Wild Horse Annie and the Last of the Mustangs*, 2013).

If Johnston felt shy, Marguerite quickly disarmed her, asking just enough questions but not so many as to overwhelm. Instead Marguerite parceled them out over time and many, many conversations on the phone and during in-person visits. The two women became so close in the time that Marguerite was researching her book, it wasn't surprising that some of what she wrote as Johnston's thoughts in the book were once Marguerite's own. For example, as shared previously, young Marguerite had skated to the library near her Milwaukee home, imagining herself a character in a book. Now she took those thoughts she'd had as a child and made them Johnston's "Annie" character in *Mustang*: "*Now books were my life. For these moments I skimmed across the ice with Hans Brinker...*" Johnston had also been hospitalized with polio as a child, and perhaps because the two women had both suffered life-altering illnesses in their youth, theirs seemed even more of a twinned fate.

Marguerite and Johnston had both emerged triumphant over their childhood afflictions. Both had known struggle and success, though Marguerite's life was clearly the more charmed. Unlike the rheumatic fever that had weakened Marguerite's heart and necessitated frequent rests, Johnston's bout with polio had left her permanently deformed. The two sides of her face were unmatched, thanks to the long time she'd spent in a body cast in a San Francisco hospital—something Marguerite and Robert Lougheed, *Mustang's* illustrator, would treat with great sensitivity. (The drawings in the book never show Johnston as disfigured; she's rendered as a black-and-white sketch or a faraway figure.)

Marguerite made similar adjustments to many of the facts of Johnston's life. Some of the details that seem rather of relatively little importance were "adapted" to suit her story, like how and where Johnston wrote a draft of the bill to protect wild horses for the Nevada State Legislature. In *Mustang*, Johnston's character writes the draft beside a pot-bellied stove, but as the real Johnston later recounted in a story in *The Daily Oklahoman* (September 21, 1967), the true location was a bit less suitable for a children's book. *"I didn't have a typewriter so I went over to a bar which was full of relics, borrowed a vintage L.C. Smith and sat down to a poker table. The bar owner asked the men to stop long enough for me to type the bill."* (Johnston's true-life tale was arguably more interesting than Marguerite's sanitized version—not to mention more fun.)

Johnston was also "rougher around the edges" in real life than she was depicted in Marguerite's book. It was partly by nature (she was a rancher's daughter, after all) and necessity (she was often in danger of being killed by the ranchers she angered with her Mustang work). Johnston carried a gun at all times, and she liked a stiff drink or two (or three). Her fondness for bourbon was well-documented. Marguerite, by comparison, was more of a teetotaler—although she did spend a few bleary nights with Johnston and a pitcher of Bloody Marys that left her unable to read her notes afterward. That was the end of that sort of interview, according to Cruise/Griffiths: *"On a later visit, Henry issued an edict against excessive drinking, at least until the work of interviewing and note-taking had been completed."*

The two women sent letters back and forth for months, punctuated by in-person visits. Marguerite asked detailed questions of Johnston and Johnston responded with detailed notes on her life and work. Was she essentially Marguerite's unpaid research assistant in the telling of her life story? If she was, she was certainly willing, and Marguerite emphasized her importance over and over again, often referring to *Mustang* as *"our book"* in her letters.

Before the book was published and although she had only partially finished the manuscript, Marguerite briefly considered showing Johnston some early pages on her return to Reno (something Marguerite had never done with anyone else). But she changed her mind and did not, although she did read aloud a small part of a draft when Johnston and her mother visited Wayne the following winter. Cruise/Griffiths noted that the Wayne visit, while pleasant, had caused Johnston to *"suffer a few pangs"* upon seeing the comfortable life that Sid and Marguerite led—not to mention their closeness. The latter was particularly painful after Johnston's recent loss of her husband. *"...it was Sid's and Marguerite's obvious affection for each other after 45 years of marriage that most reminded Velma of what she no longer had."*

The two women shared another bond that was oddly unremarked-upon by either one of them. Both had given up beloved horses—Johnston gave up her beloved buckskin Mustang Hobo (she became allergic to horses later in life) when she sold her ranch and moved into town to live with her mother. Hobo ended up living nearby but Johnston rarely visited. Marguerite gave Friday to the owner of a nearby stable when it came time for him to have a place to retire. But both women kept mementos from their riding days: Johnston had Hobo's bridle and Marguerite kept Friday's saddle, which she took to California when she and Sid moved to Rancho Santa Fe a few years later. (In a recorded 1968 "Meet the Authors" interview produced by Imperial International Learning, Marguerite also mentions buying a Mustang of her own when she was Out West, but the ownership was brief—she donated the horse to the Cowboy Hall of Fame.)

A New Artist Partner

Marguerite wrote much of *Mustang* while she and Sid were vacationing at the Camelback Inn & Resort Spa in Scottsdale, Arizona. If she couldn't have a horse, pony, or burro in her backyard as her inspiration, at least she could write with a view of the mountains and the Sonoran desert—in the comfort of a posh resort. Camelback was a regular destination for Marguerite and Sid; they'd vacationed there regularly for years so that Sid could escape the Midwestern winter and play golf. (Marguerite occasionally played golf as well, though far less skillfully, she admitted, than Sid.)

While Marguerite was researching and writing *Mustang*, Canadian-born artist Robert Lougheed was producing the paintings that would bring her words to even greater life. Lougheed, who started out as Robert and became "Bob" to Marguerite in their letters as their relationship deepened, had arrived fairly late to the project; in fact, Marguerite was already halfway through writing the book when Lougheed signed on as its illustrator in 1966. (Had Marguerite held out hope that she and Dennis might somehow be able to create one last book together?)

When he agreed to illustrate *Mustang*, Lougheed was already a well-established artist. At the time, he and his wife were living in the small town of Newton, Connecticut, in the western half of that state, working out of a studio barn when he wasn't traveling to paint. Like Dennis, Lougheed had a few horses and liked to paint on location. In fact, he spent many months traveling in the American West with his wife Cordelia (aka Cordy), until they eventually moved to New Mexico.

When Marguerite first approached Lougheed about illustrating *Mustang*, he turned her down. He wasn't an illustrator but a painter, Lougheed informed Marguerite, whose response was equal parts flattery and practical suggestion. Lougheed could illustrate her book with full-size paintings that Rand McNally would size to the book, and Lougheed could later sell his work to art galleries. Marguerite, the savvy marketer, was right about that; Lougheed later sold several of the paintings to Henry Ford II, who in turn donated them to the Cowboy Hall of Fame in Oklahoma City (now the National Cowboy & Western Heritage Museum), where they reside alongside the work of famed Western painters like Remington and Russell.

Once he agreed to the project, Lougheed's illustrations progressed quickly. He had hundreds of photographs of Mustangs that he'd taken during his travels that he used as references, and his knowledge of the American West, and of its Mustangs, was considerable, as he'd spent so much time traveling around painting the canyons, the prairies, and the deserts. Lougheed cared deeply about wild horses—almost as deeply as Johnston. In his letters to Marguerite, Lougheed shared his own often impassioned thoughts about the importance of Mustangs in settling the American West. It was truly remarkable luck that Marguerite had managed to find in Lougheed an artist as gifted as Wesley Dennis, and one whose appreciation and depth of knowledge about horses also exceeded her own. Lougheed and Marguerite became good friends, although there was no replacing Dennis in her heart.

When *Mustang* was published, Lougheed was not only pleased by the reproductions of his work but even declared to Marguerite: *"Never have my drawings been reproduced so well... the whole layout of the book delights me."* Their first partnership was such a success that they not only teamed up for a second—*San Domingo: The Medicine Hat Stallion*—but Lougheed, his wife Cordy, and Marguerite took a trip to Wyoming in the Lougheed family camper, a daring adventure for a seventy-year-old writer who was doing less and less arduous travel.

Safeguarding Freedom

When Johnston finally received a copy of *Mustang* at the end of September in 1966 (sent by Marguerite some months before the book's official publication), she wrote Marguerite a hugely emotional note, one that Johnston said had taken her a great deal of time and effort to craft. *"I have my emotions under control now which was far, far from the case last Monday from the moment I received Mustang until late into the night when I was finally able to get to sleep.... It is beautifully written, Marguerite. What a loving, living tribute to Charley! As for my dad—who grieved from the time of his son's death until his own that the Bronn family name would die with him—how proud he would be for the touch of glory given to it by two women who share a pair of moccasins."* (Marguerite and Johnston had exchanged gifts of hand-tooled moccasins after Marguerite had thanked Johnston for allowing her to "walk" in her moccasins in writing the book.)

Mustang: Wild Spirit of the West proved a great critical as well as popular success. Flattering profiles of Marguerite appeared in papers all over the country. *"Marguerite Henry writes UP to children,"* announced the headline of a profile of Marguerite by Sheri Graves in *The Press Democrat* of Santa Rosa, California (November 20, 1966). The headline was plucked from a quote by Marguerite as to how she approached writing for young readers. *"Children want to believe what they read. They don't pick up a book with tongue in cheek but out of curiosity and hunger. This puts you on your mettle. You have to have the facts—to write UP to children,"* Marguerite said.

In the same interview, Marguerite made a surprising confession. She didn't just write her books out of love for children or animals (and particularly horses) but also because she wanted to earn her own money. *"Even when I was a child, I felt this way... Even now, I can't take money from my husband. I have to earn my own."* It's a startling revelation from a long-married woman whose husband made a more than comfortable living, but it was (further) evidence of just how independent Marguerite was, and yet another example of how different her life was from most women of her age and era.

Marguerite made one more revealing, or perhaps self-deprecating, admission during that same interview when she recalled having recently read some of her earliest work, written when she was eleven years old and when she wrote *"a column for a newspaper"* (likely the oft-noted magazine story). *"I read it now, and I'm amazed—it's better than what I write now!"* Marguerite was writing what she called *"adult love stories"* back in those days; she didn't begin to write stories for children until she had grown up.

It was just a month after Dennis's death when Marguerite was out on the road with the *Mustang* book tour, barnstorming her way through book signings around the country, from Ohio department stores to Nevada bookstores where readers were invited to attend "autograph parties" to have Marguerite sign both her old and new books. This time there was no Dennis, but she did have Johnston as her cheerleader and champion, and Johnston promoted the book as if it were her own.

Marguerite made more stops in the Midwest and far West as her book tour continued, but by December she was back closer to home, signing books in Minnesota, where she was distressed to find very few young children who actually knew much about horses. She was particularly taken aback when a young boy attending her "autograph party" for *Mustang* in Minneapolis said, upon seeing the title, *"Hey, look, here's a story about a car!"*

In the years that followed the book's publication Johnston continued her work on behalf of the Mustangs (while defying more attempts on her life by vengeful ranchers) until she died of cancer in 1977 at the age of sixty-five. It was just over ten years after *Mustang* was published. At the time of her death, Johnston was still living in the small house that she and her mother had shared—the same one that Marguerite described so poignantly as *"a little house on a hill with the spangly lights of Reno spilling like jewels far below"* in *Mustang*. Perhaps the ending of the book fits as her epitaph: *"And somewhere in their rimrocks and mesas wild horses kick up their heels, magnificent in the freedom that is theirs because Annie and thousands of everyday people worked to safeguard it."*

In a sad coda to all Johnston's efforts on behalf of Mustangs, the work of saving them continues to this day, against equally fierce resistance. As of this writing, the BLM (Bureau of Land Management) still rounds up wild horses and burros via helicopters—the same inhumane methods Johnston lobbied against. And some seventy thousand wild horses and burros are languishing in BLM holding centers, which are, by many accounts, overcrowded and unsafe. The work continues long after Wild Horse Annie's fighting days.

letters

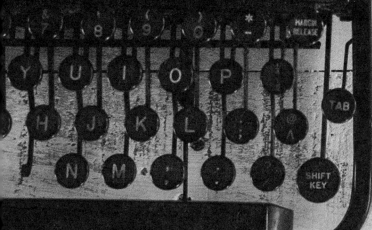

Sunday

Dearest Gee Gee —

I still love you even if I don't write. In Apache Junction Ariz. recently I yearned to send you a card, but didn't have your address with me. Wish you had a simple one like Wayne, Ill.!

Anyway never doubt that I'm un-mindful of your problems. Think of you loads and hope your writing goes along easier'n mine. Yours ever,

Marguerite Maxwell

14

SAN DOMINGO:
THE MEDICINE HAT
STALLION

14

"Sometimes his happiness with Domingo frightened him.
It seemed too great to keep."

—

FROM *SAN DOMINGO*

(FIRST PUBLISHED 1972)

Accordingto Marguerite, the inspiration for *San Domingo* was a boy named Andy Burke (a pseudonym) whose teacher wrote Marguerite a letter that about broke Marguerite's heart. It was, as the teacher Blanche Wilson said to Marguerite, an all-too-common story of a violent father, a terrible home life, and a frightened son. Andy's home life was brutal, said the teacher, who noted that Andy had a *"drunken father"* who had recently terrorized his children by threatening to kill them for fun. *"This boy, Andy, and his sister escaped by hiding under a mattress."* Then the father had cruelly given away Andy's beloved horse.

After reading Wilson's letter, Marguerite sent her a copy of her book *All About Horses* (1962) to give to Andy. The boy responded with a heartfelt letter to Marguerite, which his teacher said took him three days to write during school recess hour. The letter described all the things he and his beloved Palomino horse did together, and the fun they'd had, riding up and down the hills, his little dog beside them. Then Andy delivered the crushing news: *"My father sold my horse while I was at school and I did not want him to go. My mother said that he would not go into the trailer without me or my little dog… so now I draw pictures of him in school. (Signed) Your friend, Andy Burke."*

Marguerite recounted Andy's story in the essay "A Weft of Truth and a Warp of Fiction," and the years afterward that the letter haunted her. *"Try as I might I couldn't wash the Burke family out of my consciousness,"* Marguerite wrote. She wanted to think of a story that she might write to bring Andy some measure of happiness, and that story eventually became the book *San Domingo*.

The real boy's pain and loss, and his cruel father, were transformed into the fictional Peter Lundy and his own cruel father, a Medicine Hat stallion named San Domingo, and a (real-life) Irishman, who was Peter's one true friend. It was a story that Marguerite hoped Andy might read one day and that might bring him some peace. ("Medicine Hat" horses have a white face with a colored marking that covers their ears and head. This coloration is rare and was prized in Native American tribes where such horses were believed to have special powers.)

The Oshoto Express

The research that Marguerite undertook in the writing of *San Domingo* was some of the most physically taxing of her writing career. She traveled to Wyoming with Lougheed and his wife Cordy in a camper (dubbed "Oshoto Express") to research the route of the Pony Express riders (the mail service that relied on relays of horse-mounted riders from 1860 to 1861) that would become the focal point of the book, and to meet Robert Brislawn, an Irish horseman with whom she'd been corresponding for many months. The trip marked the real beginning of the friendship between writer and artist, as well as between Robert Brislawn and Marguerite.

When Marguerite met Robert Brislawn in Oshoto, Wyoming, she was utterly captivated by the man's almost magical ability with horses. In a letter to her editor Mary Alice Jones, dated October 20, 1967, Marguerite described how she and Lougheed and Brislawn watched a herd of horses galloping toward them. *"They were flying toward Robert Brislawn, the gentle little crickety old man in a high-crowned cowboy hat that all but swallows him."* It's a look that Lougheed captured perfectly—and a hat that Brislawn (aka "Brisley," as Marguerite later called him) gave to Marguerite, who in turn gave it to Sid. Brislawn owned one hundred and thirty-five horses that roamed his four thousand acres, and it was in his company that Marguerite learned that a Medicine Hat pony was a rare thing. It was Brislawn's Medicine Hat stallion San Domingo who became the equine star of her next book and the inspiration of the book's title.

When Marguerite wrote an introduction to *The Way of the Irish Horseman* by Neil UiBreaslin (the son of Robert Brislawn—this was his preferred spelling of his family's last name), she described how she and Brislawn had exchanged letters before they met in person. *"Our letters were filled with mutual respect, I for his wisdom and he for my thirst for learning."* It was upon meeting Brislawn that Marguerite realized he was exactly who she needed to provide a center for her book; he was the true, authentic hero, the embodiment of the spirit of the horsemen who settled the West. He might also have been the emotional successor to Grandpa Beebe. *"Brislawn was fluent in English, Gaelic and Horse,"* Marguerite said (the latter of course was the highest compliment).

The real-life Robert Brislawn (or Robert O'Breaslain, as he appears in Marguerite's dedication—his family seem to have been men of many monikers) was a highly regarded horseman who fought to preserve the history and lineage of the Spanish Barb horse. He was an articulate, well-educated man, as evidenced by the "Sketch of the Life of Bob Brislawn and the Spanish Mustang" that he wrote and sent to Marguerite, but like Grandpa Beebe, he became a good deal more folksy on the pages of her book: *"How about if'n I throw in Billy-goat and Nanny?"* and *"Well, I'll be hogtied,"* and *"I figger."*

Once their work on *San Domingo* began, Marguerite's letters to Lougheed reveal that writer and artist discussed the fit of the illustrations to the text, just as she and Dennis once had. *"As I remember we suddenly agreed on the endpapers—that great wide landscape and a tiny rider hellbent across the vastness,"* she wrote. The party of three—Marguerite, Lougheed, and his wife Cordy—traveled the winding route of the Pony Express as Marguerite took pictures, hundreds and hundreds of pictures of landmarks and way stations. Back home in Wayne, Marguerite tracked down every book and pamphlet and article on the Pony Express that she could find in libraries, museums, and bookstores. It wasn't a chore—it was an extension of the joy she'd felt on (yet another) research trip, which turned out to be the last such big trip she ever took. *"All of these preliminaries I am enjoying to the full, letting the pieces fall into place before beginning on the actual writing,"* Marguerite wrote.

Not everything about the production was seamless; Lougheed delivered many more illustrations than he'd originally been commissioned to create, both black-and-white and color. He wasn't happy with the ratio of work to payment and complained to Marguerite that the number of illustrations he'd been commissioned to make was much smaller than the number that he produced for the book. Marguerite replied, in effect, that he could petition Rand McNally but that her hands were tied—and had he considered joining a guild of artists and writers?

Tiffs Over Titles

There were also problems with the published book, specifically the title. Marguerite was not happy with it, according to Catherine McClure, whose father "Spec" McClure was a Los Angeles based writer for Walt Disney Studios who became Marguerite's friend and sometime advisor. Marguerite wanted Peter Lundy's name in the title—and she also liked the title "Orphans Preferred," which were the words of the handbill published by the United States Postal Service to recruit young riders to deliver the mail during the eighteen months the Pony Express existed. The bill (in full) read: *"Wanted: Young, Skinny, Wiry Fellows not over 18. Must be willing to risk death daily. Orphans preferred."*

But Rand McNally's chosen title stood.

It wasn't the first, or the last, title battle that Marguerite would lose. She had also wanted "Wild Horse Annie" to be the title of *Mustang: Wild Spirit of the West* (as had Johnston), and she disliked the title *The Illustrated Marguerite Henry* for the book that featured profiles of her favorite illustrators and partners. She wanted it to be titled "My Loves"—a title far more personal than the one her publisher chose.

When *San Domingo* was published, Lougheed seemed to have forgotten his dissatisfaction with payment in his admiring letter to Marguerite: *"...I have come to know Peter, his father and mother almost as well as I know this unforgettable character, Brisley. We shall remember him as long as we live, and you have made him live for long years to come. These illustrations have again turned into twice thirty* [meaning sixty] *but I do hope they are close to what you had hoped for, and may help to decorate this fine piece of writing."* Lougheed even accompanied Marguerite on some book signings, and on at least one occasion (in Topanga, California) brought the original oil painting of San Domingo along. Sometimes he did book signings solo as well.

The reviews of *San Domingo* were largely positive. Elizabeth Coolidge of *The Boston Globe* (February 3, 1973) was particularly impressed: *"Like any fine novelist, Marguerite Henry has woven together many threads in her newest novel. There is the incomparable Indian pony, for she is THE writer of books about horses for children."* Coolidge also wrote that she'd asked Marguerite about the Dalmatian Dice who features in San Domingo, and Marguerite replied that he was named after Wesley Dennis's favorite Dalmatian, whom the waggish Dennis liked to tell children was *"clean but not spotless."* When Marguerite mentioned Dennis, Coolidge took the opportunity to note that while replacing Wesley Dennis seemed *"impossible,"* Lougheed was a worthy successor whose oils *"have the Western feel of Remingtons."*

Other reviewers were equally generous in their assessment. Luvada Kuhn, writing in the *Chillicothe Gazette* of Ohio on June 30, 1973, found *San Domingo* to be of the same caliber of *King of the Wind*. *"She is, in this reviewer's opinion, the best writer of horse stories, bar none."* A reviewer for *The Chicago Tribune* (November 5, 1972) called *San Domingo* Marguerite's *"best in many years"* and found *"more depth in characterization than most fiction by Marguerite Henry,"* a note of mixed praise but more complimentary than a reviewer for the *Austin American* (Texas), who was a bit less impressed, writing on December 10, 1972, that *"horsiness"* was emphasized in the book, making it attractive to both boys and girls, but that the book *"lacks humor and the dialogue is somewhat stilted, but this is perhaps expected and even required to lend the book an atmosphere of 'good old days.'"*

Did Andy Burke, the boy who inspired Marguerite to write *San Domingo,* ever read the book? There is no note from Marguerite about whether or not she sent him a copy by way of his teacher. But Marguerite did get one of her preferred titles when the book was reissued. In its later incarnation it was retitled *Peter Lundy and the Medicine Hat Stallion,* and it was made into a made-for-television movie by the same name in 1978.

Leaving Mole Meadow

After some forty years in their Mole Meadow home, Marguerite and Sid made a surprising move. They sold the ranch house in Wayne and bought a ranch house in Rancho Santa Fe, California in what Art Richardson recalled had seemed a rather speedy fashion. One day they were simply gone. The reason given for their move was Sid's health and his wish to play golf all year 'round. Furthermore, they'd spent so many winters in the West, it seemed like a natural next step, and Rancho Santa Fe was another "mink and manure" community where horses and money were both plentiful, but unlike Wayne, the ocean, which Marguerite loved, was nearby as well.

Marguerite and Sid sold the much-loved "Mole Meadow" to a Chicago-based decorator named Edward Kershaw who lived in the home for several years before he passed away in 1979 at seventy-five years of age, leaving no survivors. His estate sold the house after his death. (As an interesting aside, Kershaw was related, by way of marriage—his brother's wife's sister—to well-known actors Louise Campbell and her husband Horace McMahon, famous for his performance in the *Naked*

City television series (aired 1958 to 1963). This association—however distant—must surely have pleased aspiring thespian Marguerite.)

It was hard to believe that after a lifetime spent in the Midwest, Marguerite simply pulled up stakes and started her life over so far from home. How could she leave a place that she described as one where *"things happen by magic"* to people? But Marguerite's life in Wayne in 1970 was much changed from the early halcyon days. There were no more pony birthday parties with hundreds of children in attendance. Misty was gone—as were Jiggs and Friday, who, after Marguerite gave him away, passed away of old age at the Shade n' Oak stable. (When he died, the stable's owner Eddie Pacuinas brought Marguerite a bit of Friday's black tail, which Marguerite hung on a wall in her studio.)

Without the parties and the children and horses, or even visits to Chicago and her editor Mary Alice Jones (who had long since moved south to Nashville, where she worked on behalf of the Methodist Church), there were now only ghosts of Marguerite's once exciting and adventurous life. Perhaps that was another reason why Marguerite wanted to start over again somewhere far away—not just Sid's failing health and his wish to play golf. She needed to be somewhere new to write the last chapter of her life.

Marguerite and Sid settled into a small green ranch house set amongst towering eucalyptus trees high on a hill. The house came with a pool and a pool house that Marguerite soon commandeered for her studio. *"I live high on top of a mountain and I have a studio in the middle of a paddock,"* Marguerite told an interviewer, slightly embellishing the truth. (The horse paddocks belonged to her neighbors who lived just below.)

She wrote cheerfully of their new home in the West. *"We are both swimming the days away and making the most of them before the weather dives from 84 degrees to the 70s and 60s,"* Marguerite wrote to Alberita

Semard. The two women had been close for many years, long before Marguerite and Sid left for California. *"Just the sight of your handwriting gives my heart a pang and a glow,"* Marguerite wrote to Semard on a post-card dated June 8, 1960, when she and Sid were still living in Wayne. Semard, a columnist and longtime writer for *The Chicago Tribune*, had also been good to Marguerite professionally, having written a glowing review of *Black Gold* in 1957, soon after the book was published. (Although she was six years Marguerite's senior, Semard outlived her by six years. She passed away in Chicago at the astonishing age of 107.)

Marguerite also remained very close to her Chicago-based Rand McNally executive publisher Bennet Harvey and his wife Dorothy. Marguerite and Harvey were regular correspondents—even confi-dantes. In a letter addressed *"Dear Dorothy and Bennet,"* Marguerite admitted that the move to Rancho Santa Fe might have been a mis-take. *"How I envy your wisdom in not moving to California or Flori-da or the Carolinas for 'the golden years,'"* she confided. *"Toward the last, Sid was obsessed with the yearning to go home. Whether this meant Wayne or his parents' home I don't know but there was pleading and puzzlement in his eyes when I'd say, 'But Sid, we are home.'"* Margue-rite added a consoling (perhaps for herself?) note. *"We did have some good years with Sid swimming and golfing and best of all, enjoying our wonderfully staffed library."*

There were a few other positive attributes to living in such a tucked-away location in Rancho Santa Fe, Marguerite admitted to other friends. For example, she didn't lock her doors and even had an unusual method of determining whether her house had been entered by another while she was away: Every time Marguerite went out to lunch or a meeting, she left a ten-dollar bill on a table by the door. If the money was still there when she returned, Marguerite knew that her house had not been burgled.

The move to Rancho Santa Fe came just before *San Domingo* was published and a year before Misty died in her sleep on Chincoteague. At the time of Misty's death, her only remaining foal, Stormy, was in the stall next door. Misty's two earlier foals Little Wisp and Phantom Wings—neither of whom ever gained the fame of their sibling—had died of silage poisoning within days of one another in 1964, as reported in *The Morning News* of Wilmington, Delaware. (Silage can be toxic to horses if mold and other bacteria develop in the feed.) Maureen Beebe was back in Chincoteague, having returned just two years earlier with her two daughters after the death of her husband Gary Hursh. Misty's death was covered in newspapers around the country and by the wire services too. *"She was like a member of our family,"* Ralph Beebe said.

Ralph Beebe later explained why he decided to have Misty stuffed, mounted, and displayed at his ranch after her death. It was *"so children can enjoy her,"* Beebe said. A story on the subject appeared in *The Sacramento Bee* on October 18, 1972, with a rather alarming headline: *"Even After Death Misty Will Stand in Her Stall."* The same story in the *Index-Journal* of Greenwood, South Carolina, featured a headline that was yet more succinct: *"Famous Horse to Be Stuffed."* Marguerite was said to have been horrified by the idea of a "stuffed Misty," but her thoughts on the subject were not sought by reporters—or least they were never mentioned in print.

Ralph Beebe died soon after he expressed this desire, and it fell to his wife Jeanette to have Misty stuffed. It required two different taxidermists—a second one to fix the botched job of the first. Misty the stuffed pony was placed in a small one-story cinderblock building with "Home of Misty" painted in red letters on the side. There were two rooms in this "Misty Museum": one where tourists paid a fifty-cent admission and one where Misty stood *"life-like but motionless in a stall carpeted with imitation straw*," according to Donald Kimelman in *The Baltimore Sun* (August 4, 1975). Kimelman described in detail (perhaps too much detail) how and why Misty had to be taxidermized twice. Apparently the first taxidermist had cut Misty into pieces then abandoned the project. The second taxidermist (Charles Oxenham) stepped in and *"pieced it together and stretched it artfully over a metal and plaster skeleton."*

While some of the visitors to the ranch were happy to see Misty, others were far less enchanted. A young girl from Massapequa, New York, was reportedly left "disconsolate" at the sight. The Misty Museum was a joint endeavor between the Beebes and Greg Merritt, who ran the Chincoteague Miniature Pony Farm next door (which is long since gone). Mr. Merritt told *The Sun*: *"Most horses, I'd say bury them. But a horse as special as Misty, where the book still sells so many copies a year, I think it's important that kids should see her and know she was real."*

Apparently, Ralph Beebe had hoped to have Misty's offspring stuffed and put on display at the farm as well, but Jeanette was working as a clerk in a gift shop at the time, and she couldn't afford to completely carry out his wishes (only Stormy was stuffed too). It seemed to be the end of the Misty era, although it turned out to be the end of just one of *many* eras—Misty and stuffed Stormy now reside in the Chincoteague Museum along with other relics of the Chincoteague past. The museum purchased the Beebe ranch for $625,000 in June 2023 with the hope to eventually transfer Misty and Stormy to the premises.

Misty's Twilight

Marguerite continued to write and to give interviews and answer the still-endless letters that she received from children when she entered her eighties, although her life slowed dramatically with Sid's decline, and she spent more and more time caring for him. The books that followed *San Domingo* were largely retrospective rather than original stories (*The Pictorial Life Story of Misty; The Illustrated Marguerite Henry*) and a complete revision of *The Little Fellow* without the offensive phrasing of the first. For some time, Marguerite stopped working in her studio, though she returned to the studio after Sid's death in 1987.

By then Marguerite's health was fragile as well but she managed one final sequel in the Misty series. That book, *Misty's Twilight*, published in 1992, is based on the true story of a dermatologist named Sandy Price who traveled to Chincoteague to buy a descendant of Misty and her foal (Twilight) who grew up to become a champion dressage pony. Misty's Twilight (aka Twi) had to overcome prejudice against her "lowly" pony status. The real Twilight went on to have several foals and lived to a very ripe old age (thirty-one). She passed away in 2009. Although Marguerite never met Twi, as her health no longer allowed her to travel by then, she carefully researched the book as she had with so many projects before, sending Price checklists of questions about Twi, to which Price sent detailed replies.

While Marguerite still received dozens of fan letters almost daily, the days when she appeared on the front pages of local newspapers were long in the past. She didn't even rate top billing in a local reading in 1974 promoted as an "Author-Go-Round," which featured conversations with writers chatting with local children. Marguerite was mentioned almost in passing, given less ink than Frank Bonham, "a third-generation Californian with more than 500 short stories and articles." Marguerite was simply noted as a Southern California resident "best known for her horse stories" and her Newbery Award for *King of the Wind*. The other featured writers were much younger than Marguerite. Bill Peet was a writer for Disney and Zilpha Keatly

Snyder was the author of three books that earned Newbery Honors, and her books—including *The Egypt Game, The Headless Cupid,* and *The Witches of the Worm*—were of an entirely new generation of children's literature.

letters

Lauren Bulone
13135 Cimarron Circle South
Largo, FL 33774
September 29, 1999

Marguerite Henry
C\0
Scholastic Publishing Company
555 Broadway
New York City N.Y 10012

Dear Ms. Henry :

In school I am reading the book **Brown Sunshine** and I love it because it is about horses. I love horses and I have one of my own. I haven't finished reading the whole book yet, but I think it is really good so far. You seem to know a lot about horses from what I've read so far. Do you have a horse of your own? Is Brown Sunshine a real horse? Where did you get the idea for the book?

I like how you use detail and description in your books. That to me is the sign of a great author.

I hope you can write back to me soon.

Sincerely,

Lauren M. Bulone

15

BROWN SUNSHINE
OF SAWDUST VALLEY

15

*"Brown Sunshine with the sensitive ears and the bouncy tail
grew to enjoy the sameness of his days. Early each morning
the sun woke him, warming his coat first
and then his bones underneath."*

—

FROM *BROWN SUNSHINE OF SAWDUST VALLEY*
(FIRST PUBLISHED 1996)

Marguerite's final book, *Brown Sunshine of Sawdust Valley,* was published the year before her death, although it was a book that was several decades in the making. Marguerite had been thinking about mules as far back as 1949 when she was looking for material on the "mule chapter" of her reference book *Album of Horses* and kept notes over the years. And of course she'd ridden mules during her Grand Canyon expeditions while writing *Brighty.* But it took mule artist Bonnie Shields to bring the full mule world into Marguerite's life.

Shields recalled first meeting Marguerite and Sid in the late 1970s, during the "Mule Day" celebrations in Columbia, Tennessee—an event that began as a one-day parade and mule show and evolved into a multi-day spectacle. Shields (aka "Bonnie Shields the Tennessee Mule Artist") was not only a mule artist but a mule owner and mule devotee—and by her admission, a "gushing fan" of Marguerite's.

Shields recalled that first meeting in highly specific detail. "I was your typical horse crazy girl. I grew up on her [Marguerite's] books," Shields recalled in a phone conversation from her Idaho home.

Marguerite had found Bonnie's "mule friends" via the Tennessee librarians who were helping with her mule research for her current book project. Shields had been living in Tennessee at the time and her "mule friends" arranged the meeting between the two women. "That's how she worked. They knew her," said Shields. "I recall they gave me a date and gave me the name of the motel. I remember it was a sunny morning. I ended up chatting with Marguerite in her second-floor motel room while sitting on a motel bed with Marguerite. Sid sat nearby and didn't say a word." Shields told Marguerite how much she loved her books, and the two women pledged to stay in touch—and they did for years, writing letters back and forth. But Marguerite was busy with other books and Sid's by-then failing health.

By the mid-1980s, Shields met "a man from Bishop, California" and moved west, and happily, much closer to Marguerite, with whom she renewed a friendship, visiting as often as she could—often for a lunch ("sandwiches—Marguerite didn't cook") and a swim. Marguerite was determined to finally write the "mule book," said Shields. "We sat down, and she started talking about ideas—asking me what I thought. She had a big yellow sheet of paper." Marguerite began writing the book, but put it aside once more. When she finally finished the story, it took a few years for it to be published. Then there was the issue of the illustration on the cover. "They wanted a long-eared Arabian horse,"

/ 122–124 /
Although the sign outside the Museum of Chincoteague
Island in Chincoteague, Virginia, invites passers-by to
"visit" the beloved Misty, they will find only "stuffed"
versions of Misty and her famous filly Stormy within.

◆ *Photos © Lettie Teague*

/ 125 /

The building that was once the barn Marguerite had built for Misty, Friday, and Jiggs behind her house in Wayne, Illinois. It has long since ceased to be home for horses and is now an artist's studio.

✦ *Photo © Lettie Teague*

/ 126 /

Mary Jon Quayle Edwards, one of the Wayne neighborhood children and part of the Quayle family who lent Marguerite their barn when baby Misty first arrived in Illinois, is now in her eighties and still riding every day—and teaching riding too. Here she is with one of her horses RiverMist—aka Misty, of course!

✦ *Photo © Lettie Teague*

Shields said, referring to the publisher. And by then Marguerite was dealing with heart problems that had shadowed her all her life.

Brown Sunshine is a sweet, rather simple story about a horse-crazy young girl who wants a horse desperately but whose father can only buy her an old mare that later gives birth to a foal, who turns out to be a mule. The attending vet is a kindly, knowledgeable fellow named Doc Winquist (a nod to Marguerite's old Wayne riding master friend). After a few minor problems and some snobbish people who don't care for mules, Brown Sunshine ends up wearing the crown in the Mule Days parade—and all is well.

Changing Hands

The same year that *Brown Sunshine* was (finally) published by Simon & Schuster, in 1996, the Misty of Chincoteague Foundation began raising money to build a real Misty Museum. According to a piece in the *Salisbury Daily Times* (July 21, 1996), Marguerite gave a "major" portion of a private seventy-five-thousand-dollar grant, although she hadn't set foot on the island in decades. (By then Marguerite had had several strokes, the last of which left her bedridden.) In an ugly footnote to the ongoing "stuffed Misty situation," a legal battle resulted in Misty being "carted off the island" and stuck in a shed in Newport News, Virginia, along with Stormy. She was to be kept out of public view until her "ratty hide" could be repaired.

Simon & Schuster had become Marguerite's publisher thanks to a series of sales, beginning with Rand McNally's children's book division going to MacMillan, followed by the purchase of MacMillan by Simon & Schuster. There are currently nineteen Marguerite Henry titles in print (excluding the various boxed sets) with Simon &

Schuster—impressive, perhaps, but a fraction of the fifty-nine books Marguerite wrote.

Marguerite's books still perform well all these years later, with *Misty of Chincoteague* outselling them all. Jon Anderson, President of the Children's Publishing division of Simon & Schuster, estimated that some fifty thousand copies of *Misty* are sold each year. Anderson noted that some of Marguerite's books had fallen out of copyright by the time the company acquired her work. Equally daunting was the fact that they couldn't find any of the original artwork for any of the books. It wasn't uncommon for publishers to dispose of illustrations after they had been utilized in a book. "It was treated as work for hire, and a lot of times it ended up in files or destroyed," he said.

Anderson discovered what he characterized as Marguerite's "very unusual deal" with Wesley Dennis that she made at the time of their partnership, giving him a share of the profits on the books they produced together. Simon & Schuster renegotiated the contract and set it up so that Dennis's heirs would receive royalties from her book sales.

It turned out that the Dennis artwork featured in all the original Rand McNally books had been stored in a warehouse in Wisconsin, just north of Chicago, until the 1990s, according to the Virginia art dealer John Palmer. When Rand McNally stopped publishing children's books, an unnamed representative of the publishing house notified Morgan Dennis, the son of Wesley Dennis, that he could pick up the artwork—even though Rand McNally legally owned it all. The late Mr. Palmer, born in Warrenton, and his wife Lil (who both died in 2013) owned an antique store in Virginia and were friends with Morgan Dennis. What is known is that Dennis and Palmer flew to Chicago, rented a car, picked up all the Dennis artwork stored in the warehouse, and drove back to Virginia. Many of the illustrations were sold after Palmer's death.

The Days of Patrick Henry

Although Marguerite gave up horse ownership when she and Sid moved to Rancho Santa Fe, she did have a dog, and her very last dog, a black standard poodle named Patrick Henry, arrived in a manner worthy of a Marguerite Henry story. According to Marguerite's friend and former Rancho Santa Fe neighbor Susan Foster, who became close to Marguerite in her final years, Patrick began as a "part-time" dog for Marguerite, who shared him with a neighbor. As Marguerite was home during the day when the neighbor was absent, Marguerite took the poodle day shift. The neighbor eventually lost interest in dog altogether, and Patrick became entirely Marguerite's.

But Patrick had a habit of breaking out of the house and running away, and on one such break-out he encountered Foster and her three young children playing in their front yard. It was pure chance they were there, Foster recalled. "The FedEx man had been at her house." Patrick had navigated the fence that surrounded Marguerite's house, as well as the gate at the bottom of the hill. The telephone number on his collar led Foster to Marguerite—and a friendship instantly developed between the two women. Sid had died several years before, and Marguerite was alone, although she had a household helper and a driver whom she called Mr. McCarthy. (Marguerite had stopped driving several years after she'd fallen and broken her hip. She was so fragile that her doctor insisted that she should not drive a car.) While she was frail, she was still luminous, with "flawless skin," recalled Foster.

After a series of strokes and a stay in the local hospital, Marguerite died in her bed the day before Thanksgiving in November 1997, in her small green ranch house, surrounded by Wesley Dennis paintings and all manner of horse memorabilia, including Friday's tail and bridle— not to mention stacks and stacks of letters from young correspondents.

A small memorial was held, attended by just a few family members and friends and her dog Patrick Henry, about whom she had begun to write a book that she never finished. Marguerite was cremated and her ashes, like Sid's, were scattered in the Pacific Ocean, as had been her wish.

Patrick outlived his mistress by just a few years, living first with Marguerite's friend Catherine McClure in Marguerite's home while McClure tidied up Marguerite's affairs, and later with McClure in Los Angeles. Marguerite left her house to Scripps Hospital in San Diego, where she and Sid had received care. The house, which needed work, sold for just over $750,000; it is worth many times that amount today.

McClure, designated as the alternate trustee in Marguerite's will, made sure that Marguerite's bequests were fulfilled, including the return of the Wesley Dennis artwork that had been in Marguerite's possession. (His son Morgan Dennis actually drove from Virginia to Rancho Santa Fe to collect the art.) McClure also sent boxes of Marguerite's papers and correspondence to the Kerlan Collection in the Elmer L. Andersen Library of the University Minnesota in Minneapolis, where Marguerite had already sent manuscripts and editorial correspondence. (This was no small feat. McClure recalled it took months to locate all of the papers—some of which turned out to be in a drawer, under a bed, and inside the dishwasher in Marguerite's house. McClure even found a contract in the garage rolled up inside a box of gardening tools.)

A Life of Influence

In an obituary that ran in *The Washington Post* and was picked up by papers all over the United States, reporter Brian Mooar wrote that Marguerite had *"long ago claimed a spot among the great authors of children's books."* Mooar focused his remembrance of Marguerite's influence and works almost entirely on Misty and her descendants, as well as the people of Chincoteague. He included a quote from Marguerite, who, when asked why she wrote about horses, explained, *"It is exciting to me that no matter how much machinery replaces the horse, the work it can do is still measured in horse power...even in the space age."* The Associated Press obituary likewise mentioned Misty and Chincoteague and ran a picture of Marguerite smiling widely under a very distinctive leopard print hat—the perfect photograph.

Although *Misty of Chincoteague* was most unquestionably one of Marguerite's most consequential books, and the one that brought great attention and revenue to Chincoteague Island and its ponies, it was just one of among her remarkable oeuvre—to say nothing of the many more books she'd intended to write. Marguerite was always looking for the next good story and a fresh adventure, and she spent a lifetime following her own advice: *"Make big plans. But don't let them limit your horizon. If a side road beckons, take it. Often it will lead back onto the main road again, but meanwhile you have found the rainbow, the little window in the sky, and ever afterward your life will be brighter for its color"* (*Book Bulletin*, Chicago Public Library).

Marguerite Henry made only big plans, all of her life.

letters

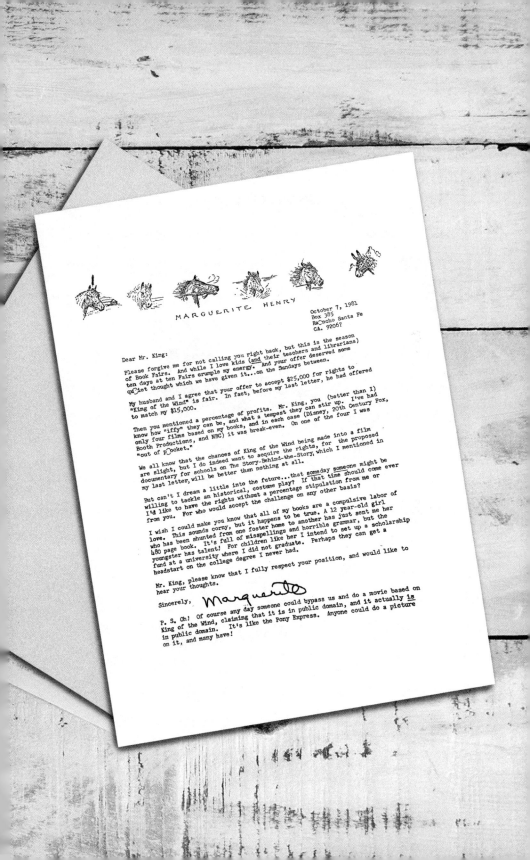

MARGUERITE HENRY

October 7, 1981
Box 385
Rancho Santa Fe
CA. 92067

Dear Mr. King:

Please forgive me for not calling you right back, but this is the season of Book Fairs. And while I love kids (and their teachers and librarians) ten days at ten Fairs crumple my energy. And your offer deserved some quiet thought which we have given it...on the Sundays between.

My husband and I agree that your offer to accept $25,000 for rights to "King of the Wind" is fair. In fact, before my last letter, he had offered to match my $15,000.

Then you mentioned a percentage of profits. Mr. King, you (better than I) know how "iffy" they can be, and what a tempest they can stir up. I've had only four films based on my books, and in each case (Disney, 20th Century Fox, Booth Productions, and NBC) it was break-even. On one of the four I was "out of pocket."

We all know that the chances of King of the Wind being made into a film are slight, but I do indeed want to acquire the rights, for the proposed documentary for schools on The Story-Behind-the-Story, which I mentioned in my last letter, will be better than nothing at all.

But can't I dream a little into the future...that someday someone might be willing to tackle an historical, costume play? If that time should come ever I'd like to have the rights without a percentage stipulation from me or from you. For who would accept the challenge on any other basis?

I wish I could make you know that all of my books are a compulsive labor of love. This sounds corny, but it happens to be true. A 12 year-old girl who has been shunted from one foster home to another has just sent me her 480 page book. It's full of misspellings and horrible grammar, but the youngster has talent! For children like her I intend to set up a scholarship fund at a university where I did not graduate. Perhaps they can get a headstart on the college degree I never had.

Mr. King, please know that I fully respect your position, and would like to hear your thoughts.

Sincerely, Marguerite

P. S. Oh! Of course any day someone could bypass us and do a movie based on King of the Wind, claiming that it is in public domain, and it actually is in public domain. It's like the Pony Express. Anyone could do a picture on it, and many have!

16

MODEL HORSES, MOVIES, AND THE UNWRITTEN BOOKS

16

*"The first Misty model was packaged in a four-color
packing case that included a softbound copy
of Misty of Chincoteague...the combination was an immediate hit."*

—

PETER STONE,
SON OF BREYER MOLDING COMPANY
CO-FOUNDER SAM STONE

Marguerite and the Model Horses

When Marguerite met Peter Stone in 1972, he was working for his family's company, the Breyer Molding Company, based in suburban Chicago. Stone was the son of Sam Stone, who had co-founded the company in 1950—with partner Charles Schiff—that would eventually become synonymous with plastic model horses. The company entered the plastic horse business almost by accident, when the F.W. Woolworth Company commissioned Breyer to produce a plastic horse to adorn a clock. That horse, known as "#57 Western Horse," proved so popular that the company immediately began receiving orders for the horse alone.

Breyer, now named Breyer Animal Creations, was sold to Reeves International in 1984 and is currently based in suburban New Jersey. Peter Stone no longer works for the company and sold his own Indiana-based model company, Stone Horses—which he owned with his wife Elaine—in 2024. Stone, now in his eighties, recalled the heady days when Breyer produced the first Misty model, which debuted in 1972, the year of the famed pony's death.

Before Stone and Marguerite met, Stone had attended toy fairs in New York where he discovered what he called "the magic of product licensing." He became convinced that his father's company should produce models of real-life horses, not just the plain, rather generic horses they were turning out. Stone was a horseman who had read Marguerite's books to his children, and he decided that her characters fit perfectly with his idea of turning real horses into models. That vision was realized by artist and model designer Christian Hess, who created the original Breyer horse, and many, many subsequent models, including the model that Stone sent to Marguerite in Wayne and later forwarded to her house in Rancho Santa Fe.

The first Misty model was packaged in a four-color packing case that included a softbound copy of *Misty of Chincoteague,* recalled Stone. The combination was an immediate hit, with sales further bolstered by an appearance in the Sears Christmas catalog—the so-called "Wish Book" of the time. There was no better place to sell a toy than the Sears catalog in the 1970s. The catalog was immense—over 1,000 pages at one point—and it was paged through by seemingly every horse-crazy boy and girl in the world. (Sears stopped publishing their catalog in 1993.)

Breyer did not advertise its models, and nor did it need to, according to Stone. Instead, Breyer models were advertised by tack shops and toy shops that touted their extensive selections in local newspaper ads. Other models inspired by Marguerite's books soon followed Misty and included Justin Morgan, San Domingo, Brighty (modeled in a reclining position), Sea Star, Brown Sunshine, Misty's Twilight, and Sham and Lady Roxana (the love interest of Sham in *King of the Wind*). All the models (save Sea Star) were tweaked and updated over the years, but it is Misty who remains a bestselling Breyer model, year in and year out.

Misty is also the model that has been "reconceived" the most often since her 1972 debut, according to Stephanie Macejko, Vice President of Marketing for Breyer Animal Creations. "The pinto markings might change over time. We did several versions," she said in a 2023 interview, adding that passionate Misty fans make a point of collecting all the many different Mistys. There is even a single gold Misty and Stormy set that Breyer produced, with the proceeds of the sale going to the Misty of Chincoteague Foundation's effort to buy the Beebe Ranch. The set sold for more than twelve thousand dollars in 2023.

While Marguerite received royalties from the use of the images and names of her horses, and the models clearly helped sell her books, how did she feel about her characters' transformation from page to plastic? The fact that boys and girls (mostly girls) who loved her stories could groom and saddle and stable their own miniature version of Justin Morgan or Misty or Sham, even if they couldn't have a real Morgan horse, Chincoteague pony, or Arabian must surely have pleased her. A plastic horse could be loved just as deeply as one that was real, and maybe one day, the child who owned it (or a whole herd of them) would grow up to have a real horse.

Marguerite would likely have been entertained to watch as, over the years, Breyer horses became much more than a hobby for horse-mad children. They are now part of an enormous festival and celebration called Breyerfest that takes place each year in Lexington, Kentucky.

Thousands of fans from all over the world converge for several days to talk about, shop for, and "show" Breyer horses. It's no exaggeration to say that Breyerfest is the Coachella of the model horse world, though its celebrations are likelier of a far tamer sort.

Marguerite and the Movies

Although Marguerite wrote fifty-nine books, a surprisingly small number of them—just five—were made into movies. When a reporter for the Carpentersville, Illinois, *Cardunel Free Press* (January 1968) declared, *"So popular are Mrs. Henry's books with young people of all ages that motion picture producers vie for the privilege of bringing them to the screen,"* that assertion owed more to hyperbole than fact. The five books that made the transition to the screen included *Misty of Chincoteague, King of the Wind,* and *Brighty,* which debuted on the big screen, and two that became made-for-television movies: *Justin Morgan Had a Horse* and *Peter Lundy and the Medicine Hat Stallion,* based on the original *San Domingo.*

Although it didn't come close to equaling the popularity of the book, the *Misty* movie, produced in 1961, proved tremendously popular for many years. The film was directed by James B. Clark (who also directed the much-beloved Cary Grant/Deborah Kerr tear-jerker *An Affair to Remember,* among other films). The *Misty* movie possessed several advantages when it debuted, the most important of which was the still-living real pony (although Misty was too old to star in the film), and then of course Marguerite, who was not only present at the filming, but also promoted the movie at every turn.

In one such effort, Marguerite wrote a piece entitled "Misty Makes the Movies," published in *Junior Libraries,* where she marveled at the production that she flew down to witness firsthand. There were three hundred extras (mostly Chincoteaguers) and one hundred and fifty ponies, plus the famed horse trainer Les Hilton *"who can run as fast as the ponies he trains,"* Marguerite wrote. *"I listened spellbound to the jargon: Quiet! Roll it!"*

The movie starred David Ladd, son of the much more famous actor Alan Ladd, who later became an MGM film executive. Filmed on location, it was less than a masterpiece with often stilted dialogue and pretty low-wattage drama. In perhaps the strangest twist of all, the pony that played Misty wasn't even a pinto pony but a very pale palomino. With all the ponies in the world, it was hard to believe that the filmmakers could not find a pony that at least *slightly* resembled Misty, and perhaps had a semblance of the fabled "map of the United States" that marked her coat? (As Marguerite wrote in *Misty of Chincoteague*: *"Like her mother, she, too wore a white map of the United States on her withers, but the outlines were softer and blended into the gold of her body."*)

Marguerite was quite disappointed by this fact and made her feelings known on more than one occasion. As she wrote in her *Junior Libraries* essay, not even one of the three Misty ponies that were required to make the movie had the same coloration as the real Misty. And one of the movie-Mistys was even a dark gray who had to have her coat bleached to more (slightly) resemble the real Misty. By contrast, Marguerite was thrilled by the performances of David Ladd as Paul Beebe and Pam Smith as Maureen Beebe. *"They are not acting at all. Each rides like the wind, each has loved a special pony and lost it in death. Their laughter and their tears are real. And they even look like Paul and Maureen!"* Marguerite declared.

The movie received generally good reviews from critics who especially seemed to have enjoyed the "naturalness" of the setting. In fact, the natural beauty of the movie—filmed on Chincoteague Island with local islanders among the cast—was arguably the true star. And the authenticity of the islanders appealed to the critics too. A reviewer for *The Roanoke World News* praised their conversation as not only authentic but one that rang with *"old English phrasing."* The *"wholesomeness"* of the movie, and the book upon which it was based, was a constant theme among reviewers as well.

The movie also gave Marguerite's book a big push, as the film was rarely cited without a mention of the story that inspired it. This helped keep *Misty* on the bestseller list for many more years. When the movie debuted, Rand McNally printed *"another million and a half copies—just waiting for the picture to burst upon the world,"* according to Edith Lindeman's breathless report for *The Richmond Times Dispatch* (May 14, 1961).

Marguerite proved to be as brilliant a salesperson for the movie as she had been her book, gamely showing up all over the country to promote the film, sometimes with Misty in tow, which always drew a crowd (and the press as well). When the "World Premiere" of the Misty movie was screened on Chincoteague Island (the Chincoteague movie theater still displays pictures of that night), the event was covered by all the local papers. *"I felt like a mother who raised a little freckle-faced kid and all of sudden it got to be an astronaut,"* Marguerite gushed to the local reporter for Maryland's *Salisbury Daily Times* (June 12, 1961). Marguerite and Wesley Dennis rode in a cart drawn by the (real) Pied Piper of the book's fame, and Misty left her hoofprints in the wet concrete in front of the Island Theater.

Interestingly, no mention was made of the fact the real Misty and the movie Misty looked nothing alike. Another Misty—"Misty II"— was also present at the premiere. She was to be a gift to First Daughter Caroline Kennedy, although the transfer never took place. (Perhaps this was because Caroline already had her own pony—a gift from then-Vice President Lyndon Johnson. The pony, named Macaroni, roamed the White House lawn freely and received quite a few fan letters of his own.)

Marguerite and Dennis teamed up to promote the *Misty* movie on many other occasions and in many other places, including Dennis's hometown, Warrenton, Virginia. A reporter for *The Evening Star* (July 18, 1961) covered the event in painstaking detail: *"Pony Club children jammed the theater, popcorn in hand and were introduced to Marguerite and Wesley."* It's hard to imagine an author and illustrator garnering that kind of attention from adolescents today—or for that matter, an author and illustrator inviting the Pony Clubbers back to their house as Dennis did. Children were told they could bring lunch and sit outside under the trees of his Wildcat Farm after the movie, and Dennis and Marguerite signed their books. A list of attendees, including local grandees, was provided by *The Evening Star* editors, who noted that Marguerite and Dennis later flew to Chincoteague for the movie screening.

It was another six years before a book by Marguerite was turned into a movie again. This time it was *Brighty of the Grand Canyon* (1967), directed by Norman Foster, who was then famous for directing Davy Crockett and Charlie Chan movies. But it was the film's producer, Stephen Booth, who was responsible for bringing Marguerite's book to the big screen. In an interview with John Bustin, entertainment editor of *The Austin American-Statesman* (June 8, 1967), Booth recounted how his wife Betty bought a copy of *Brighty* for their three young sons and how they read it aloud. All five Booths were entranced by the story. Booth wanted to make the book into a movie but was convinced that Disney owned the screen rights. *"But I kept thinking about a movie of the book, so I finally wrote Rand McNally to see who owned the rights and found out, to my amazement, that they still did,"* said Booth.

The problems began when Booth decided that in order for the film to be as authentic as possible, they needed to do all of the filming on site at the Grand Canyon. This made the film complicated—and quite expensive as well. Everything had to be brought into the canyon by muleback or helicopters, and they had to film in all four seasons, so the crew worked in blazing heat and during blizzards, in just a few months' time. The unpredictability of working with animals was a complicating factor as well. *"I don't know that I'll necessarily go after more animal stories,"* said the chastened Booth. And he did not. *Brighty* was his first and last production. The real-life Brighty (aka Jiggs), who starred in the film and was well-supplied with his favorite peppermints throughout the screening, went home to Marguerite and later to the home of "Tex" Drexler, where he remained the rest of his life.

Although *Justin Morgan Had a Horse* was Marguerite's first full-length book, it was her third book-made-into-a-movie, specifically a Disney made-for-television movie that debuted in 1972. The movie rights had actually been acquired years earlier by Disney veteran producer Harry Tytle, but Walt Disney, who had been working with Tytle, died quite suddenly in the middle of the film's development, and it had to be shelved (*Atlanta Constitution*, February 6, 1972).

The star of the movie was Don Murray, an actor later best known for his role on the long-running soap opera *Knots Landing*. Murray played Justin Morgan and his love interest was played by Lana Wood. Never mind that such a character didn't exist in the book, but then she didn't get much of a role in the movie either. Gary Crosby, son of Bing (and a horseman), played a supporting role. The film was billed as "an inspirational story with wide appeal for both children and adults" that depicted an all-American story of the hardships and triumphs of Justin Morgan (schoolmaster) and his horse. The movie received generally good reviews, although, like *Misty*, it wasn't near the equal of

Marguerite's book. (The slow-motion scenes of the racing Figure are arguably some of the best scenes in the film.)

There was a bit of clever marketing around the movie; when it debuted, several horse shows were held to coincide with the movie's airing. In Philadelphia, for example, a horsewoman named Ethel Gardner held a special show and exhibition at her Cascade Farm Stables, and some of the Morgan horses that starred in the movie were entered in the Morgan Medallion Horseshow held in August at the Ventura County Fairgrounds in California. Fairgoers were encouraged to visit the stable area to view their favorite horses and admission was free.

The next Marguerite book-made-movie was another made-for-television special, although the movie had a different name than the original edition of the book (*San Domingo*). *Peter Lundy and the Medicine Hat Stallion* (1977) was the creation of famed producer Ed Friendly, who had several hits to his name, including *Little House on the Prairie*. (As previously mentioned, a later edition of the book matched the name of the film.)

Peter Lundy was played by the then-fifteen-year-old heartthrob Leif Garrett, who was a major teen star in the 1970s and had already appeared in several films and television shows. Garrett was soon to embark on a singing career, and the movie was originally intended to be a pilot for a television series, which Garrett hoped would help further his musical career. Sadly, the network declined to commission the series, and the first Peter Lundy TV movie was also the last.

Although Marguerite's story of San Domingo had been set in Nebraska Territory, the movie was filmed on location in New Mexico, where Garrett, who did all his own riding in the movie, told an interviewer, *"I like horses a lot and can ride fairly well,"* which must have pleased Marguerite. The movie received generally positive reviews and was considered a boon for Garrett's career, which sadly soon derailed in a battle with drug addiction and alcohol abuse before the star finally got sober as a much older adult. On a happier note, the horse that played San Domingo won a Craven Award, named for Richard C. Craven, the first director of the American Humane Association. The award is given to animals who have a special ability or talent. (And notably, unlike the Misty pony of that movie, the San Domingo television character looked like the horse that Lougheed had drawn for the book.)

Perhaps it was fitting that the book that many believe to be Marguerite's very best was the last time her work would be translated into a film. Filmed in England and Turkey, the *King of the Wind* movie (1990) was produced by a consortium of no less than seven men, including Peter Davis (best known for the *Highlander* films). It costarred Richard Harris and Glenda Jackson with Navin Chowdhry as Agba. It was directed by Peter Duffell, who also directed another great horse-centric classic, *The Adventures of Black Beauty*, a series that ran for two years (1972 to 1974). *King of the Wind* was screened in very few theaters in the United States and seemed to disappear altogether soon after it was made.

Nine years before *King of the Wind's* eventual theatrical release, Marguerite had written a letter to the King Brothers film production company (October 7, 1981), offering to pay the company twenty-five thousand dollars to buy back the rights to the *King of the Wind*, which it held at the time. (She eventually paid thirty thousand dollars.) As to her percentage of the film's profits, Marguerite's reply to King was a disheartening reckoning of just how far from a windfall her experience of turning her books into movies had been. *"I've had only four films based on my books, and in each case (Disney, 20ᵗʰ Century Fox, Booth Productions and NBC) it was break-even. One of the previous four I was 'out of pocket,'"* she wrote. Marguerite sounded a pessimistic note. *"We all know that the chances of* King of the Wind *being made into a film are slight, but I do indeed want to acquire the rights for the proposed documentary for schools on the Story-Behind-The-Story, which I mentioned in my last letter will be better than nothing at all."* The movie that eventually came to be, unlike the book, was not a success. It debuted in the United Kingdom where it was produced and was little-seen in the United States.

The Unwritten Books

Penning fifty-nine books was certainly a prodigious accomplishment, but for Marguerite it wasn't enough. There were many (many) more books that she'd hoped to write. Marguerite was relentless in her quest for new ideas, searching for inspiration in books and conversations and seemingly endless newspaper articles. She jotted notes on possible topics on any sort of paper at hand, including sometimes even the pages of her own books. Even Marguerite's vacations were opportunities to research new projects; a trip to Greece with Sid turned into research for a book idea. A book about a Palomino horse? Marguerite had the notes. Could that book about a Palomino be about Roy Rogers's horse Trigger? She'd outlined that idea as well. She practically wrote an entire (unpublished) book on Miniature Horses. *"I love story-sleuthing regardless of whether I strike gold or not,"* Marguerite said and often wrote her ideas as if she was writing a letter to her sister. As Marguerite explained, *"I always use that childlike method to help me think clearer."*

Unsurprisingly, most of Marguerite's book ideas centered around horses, especially racehorses. She had a veritable post parade of possible racehorse subjects, ranging from Eclipse (as noted earlier in these pages) to Secretariat to Dan Patch. Eclipse probably came the closest to being turned into a book, or at least Marguerite seemed to have amassed the greatest volume of notes on the legendary Thorough-bred sire. The great Arabian sire Witez II was also a horse she briefly considered. The horse had a suitably dramatic life, beginning in Na-zi-occupied Poland. His name means "chieftain or prince," and he was among the horses saved by General George S. Patton, a lifelong horseman, along with other Arabians, Thoroughbreds, and the Lipiz-zaners, of course.

Marguerite worked for many years trying to figure out how to turn the story of a blind mare she'd met into a book (she traveled to Michigan to spend time with the mare in person as part of her research and corresponded frequently with the horse's owner). She did much the same for a book on "stablemates" that never appeared in print. That book was to be focused on animals who befriend another species, such as goats and horses and dogs and horses. "Horses with jobs" were also often considered—in particular, circus horses and country doctor horses (who pulled doctors' buggies in the pre-auto years).

Horses that survived terrible moments in history—like Little Commander, the horse who was the only survivor of the Battle of Little Big Horn—was another book topic that Marguerite contemplated, as was a "nursing home for horses" located on the Isle of Man that Marguerite had hoped to visit one day. But Marguerite also knew she had to be realistic about the number of quests she might undertake. As Marguerite wrote to a friend who was helping her research a book on the ponies of Norway (April 10, 1964) in another idea that never turned into a book: *"When I was ten or twelve I believed that when I grew up I could do everything all at once. Be everywhere. See everything. Now I found that I can only do one story at a time, especially when the story is so big and I have so much to learn."*

letters

March 17, 1988

Dear Marguerite Henry

I love the book that was based on Misty and Chincoteague island. and I think you are the Best writer in the world. and I think how the picture you are beautiful it was great and please keep on writer.

Your friend
Jerrid Ryan Speck

I ♥ you love

17

LOVE LETTERS
FROM READERS
AND THE LEGACY
OF MARGUERITE HENRY

CHAPTER SEVENTEEN

17

Marguerite became famous for writing bestselling children's books, but as acknowledged in the Biographer's Note at the beginning of this book, she was equally as important as a young person's favorite correspondent and confidante. Decade after decade, tens of thousands of children (and even quite a few adults) sent Marguerite letters with ideas, problems, or requests, or, in the case of a Phillip from Madison, Wisconsin, praise and a touch of skepticism. *"I read* Misty of Chincoteague, *I thought those similes were clever. Did anyone help you with those similes?"* Phillip asked.

These letters were often signed "Your fan," or "Your friend," although some correspondents were particularly bold—or confident—and signed their notes "Your number one fan," or "Your best friend," or "Your reading partner." Some correspondence ended with decidedly unsubtle orders: "Write back!" More than a few of them asked to join Marguerite's fan club, if she had one. Marguerite did not, at least not in the formal sense. Her fan club included anyone who chose to send her a note.

Whether the letters she received contained questions or commands or just simple expressions of love, Marguerite responded to every single one. She penned some of her responses in longhand on notecards or lined paper, but she also often typed her responses or had a secretary or friend do so on her behalf. Many correspondents wrote back a second and a third time, and quite a few requested Marguerite's autograph. They sent photographs too—lots and lots of photographs. The little square school class photos that were commonplace in the 1970s and 1980s spilled out of endless numbers of envelopes, usually with a child's name and age printed carefully on the back. Some photographs were annotated by the child's hometown and state, the date, and a full address.

A fan named Carrie *"from the dusty town of Ramona, CA"* sent a letter to Marguerite, along with her phone number and a line that managed to be both pessimistic and goading, *"really hoping though really doubting you might call."* One older fan named Debbie from Oklahoma sent a 1981 college photograph upon which someone had noted parenthetically *(she's engaged)* on the back. Did Marguerite write Debbie a congratulatory note? Did she call Carrie and thereby prove her wrong?

Immortalized by Books

The fan letters often referenced Marguerite's books, with her correspondents citing their favorite characters or asking questions regarding characters or aspects of the plots. Did everything really happen the way that Marguerite wrote that it did? Sometimes her correspondents just reported on how her books made them feel; some did this more succinctly than others. Michelle in Ontario wrote about *Black Gold*: *"The end was sad but I survived."* Readers also displayed an admirable willing suspension of disbelief when it came to the stories that were decades old. Long after the book *Misty of Chincoteague* was published and many decades after Misty's death, the letters about her and her story kept coming. Readers wanted to know Misty as if she was the same age as she had been in her real life with Maureen and Paul. They often asked if the three of them were still in Chincoteague. The children, the pony, and the island have achieved a kind of mythic immortality.

In the early years of Marguerite's tenure as a bestselling author, the letters were so numerous that her publisher Rand McNally funded the creation of the newsletter so often referenced in these pages as a way for Marguerite's fans to connect with their favorite author and perhaps save Marguerite from writing individual letters in response (although she still personally responded to each and every note she received). The return address on the top of the newsletter was "Mole Meadow," and it often contained a mini Wayne weather update. It might be a "A brisky, frisky day at Mole Meadow" or "A Bright April in Mole Meadow."

The newsletters were not only a fun read but also a brilliant marketing tool. The front page of the newsletter often featured tidbits of events in Marguerite's life—her travel, her research, and her work on many drafts of her books, while the back of the newsletter featured "The Story Behind the Story" of her most recently published book, which made her readers feel like privileged insiders while whetting their appetite for more Marguerite. The rest of the newsletter inevitably featured photographs of the heroes of various Marguerite books (Wild Horse Annie, for example) and her favorite illustrators (a favorite photo: Wesley Dennis depicted with cigarette in hand—a photograph that wouldn't get past censors today, but which I am privileged to share in these pages), and the reader letters that Marguerite and her publisher both chose (and were granted permission) to publish.

Some of Marguerite's correspondents were aspiring writers who wanted to know where Marguerite got her ideas or why she became a writer and how they might do the same. Kathryn in Missoula, Montana, had several questions: *"How old were you when you decided to start writing books? How were you influenced to become a writer?"* A few seemed to be aspiring book critics. *"The only thing I dislike about your books is that the ending is too close to the beginning,"* wrote twelve-year-old Joe of Batavia, Illinois. Marguerite also received many, many letters with questions about proper horse care and riding; her readers assumed she was an expert in all matters horsey. Marguerite found colorful ways to proffer advice: *"If you like music and dancing, you are going to enjoy posting to your horse's trot,"* she advised, adding, *"As you are learning don't worry if you are rising too high. It will help you catch the rhythm."* Marguerite about whips to a reader named Cathy: *"The real purpose of a whip, Cathy, is not to beat an animal but to attract his attention,"* she wrote.

Some of the questions were just fun for Marguerite to answer. *"Dear Marguerite, Please tell me how to stop thinking, dreaming, and drawing horses?"* Signed, Beth Weston, Long Beach, New Jersey. Marguerite replied, *"Dear Beth, Why stop?"*

A high school junior named Kathy wrote Marguerite a note on lined notebook paper (there were many, many such letters) catching Marguerite up on the details of her life—her plans to become a nurse, and her two horses, one of whom she hoped was pregnant. *"I'll probably never meet you but it'd be a great experience if I did,"* wrote Kathy, who signed the note "Love" and included a picture of herself.

A reader named Marie in Commack, New York, age fifteen, proposed to write Marguerite's biography and offered her credentials as a potential biographer. *"I have won many literary awards and mentions. Please say yes. I have a flair for the language,"* Marie wrote, and added the sort of note that any would-be biographer has surely thought but few have probably been brave enough to express so directly: *"P.S. This is going to take a lot of work on both of us!"*

Many letters struck a more plaintive note. Some readers wrote of sadness over family troubles or experiences of painful loss. *"I know you haven't heard from me for a while because my brother has a problem. He got a divorce."* Or a writer named Diana in Crystal Lake, Illinois, who pleaded: *"Please write back—it will mean a great deal to me to know that somebody understands the way that I feel."* There were a seemingly endless number of children who wished for and dreamed of owning a horse. They knew that Marguerite would understand how they felt; some even seemed to think that Marguerite would somehow be able to intercede—perhaps argue their case before their unyielding parents.

Marguerite replied with some version of the same story over and over again. If they really, really wanted a horse, one day that wish could come true, she reassured her readers and correspondents. Her dream of a horse of her own had been realized, even if she had to endure a very long wait—all the way up until middle age. In a letter to a reader named Caroline (April 17, 1969), who desperately wanted a horse, Marguerite wrote this consoling note: *"I had to wait to be a grownup and married before I lived in a place with enough grazing ground to keep a pony happy. I discovered that no matter how long you wait it is worth the waiting."*

Some of her correspondents just seemed to want a sympathetic ear to hear their troubles. *"We had to give my dog away because we are going to move."* Many wanted to make a more personal connection than a mere letter could furnish. *"Can I come visit you?"* Some letters were penned by adults, and often included some particularly heartbreaking piece of news, like one mother whose daughter Traci died of leukemia at age sixteen who wrote, *"I want to thank you for being kind enough to answer Traci's letters. She kept all of them. They meant a lot to her."*

Another mother wrote to Marguerite to thank her for her kindness toward her daughter Lorretta and to tell Marguerite how much her books, newsletters, and letters had helped them through difficult times. *"I especially remember when Loretta asked you if it was alright to have imaginary animal friends and you wrote her, 'The invisible kind are sometimes the most fun. They are company whenever you need them and they disappear quietly when your mind is on something else.' That is beautiful!"* the mother wrote.

Book Children

Marguerite became a regular pen pal with some children, but she became especially close to one young girl, an eleven-year-old named Eugenia Snyder ("Gee-Gee") who was living in Cleveland, Ohio, then later Chatham, New Jersey during their years of correspondence. Marguerite and Gee-Gee (whom Marguerite sometimes referred to as "First Daughter") exchanged cards and letters for several years in the 1960s.

Gee-Gee and Marguerite eventually met when Marguerite and Wesley Dennis were in Cleveland on a book-signing tour. Marguerite was in perpetual motion in those years, and her notes to Gee-Gee were penned from places all over the country in 1965 and 1966—from

Naples, Florida, to New Mexico to San Francisco to her sister's grand house in Whitefish Bay, Wisconsin. Their early letters were formal—in 1964 Marguerite signed her notes to Gee-Gee as "Marguerite," but by the next year her notes were signed "All love" from "Margo," or more often, "Mom II."

The pair exchanged confidences and thoughts about writing too. Gee-Gee, by then a young teen, was working on a book, and Marguerite encouraged her work and even asked for Gee-Gee's thoughts on her own—*White Stallion of Lipizza* and later *Mustang*. Marguerite suggested that Gee-Gee create a petition of her own on behalf of the wild horses. *"Why don't you do as Annie did; get up 2 petitions—one for all your 18 and under friends to sign and one for adults?"* Marguerite reminded Gee-Gee of the chapter in *Mustang* called "The Power of Children" and closed her note *"Fight, fight, fight with a stout heart and well of confidence."*

Although Marguerite's letters were generally light-hearted and full of plans to travel or referencing having just arrived somewhere, sometimes a certain wistfulness crept in. When Gee-Gee wrote to tell Marguerite that she thought of her on Mother's Day, Marguerite replied that *"a nice tingle went up and down my spine"* and her next few lines were decidedly poignant: *"Truth is I'd a lot rather have a daughter like you than a whole armful of book children. They can't talk back and laugh and cry. They are puppets (precious ones of course) who only say and do what you tell them to. So now in my heart of hearts I'm always going to think of you as in between a book-child and a real daughter and that makes You for me, a very special person."*

Marguerite had millions of children who were her readers, her fans, her "best friends," and then a few real-life children like Gee-Gee, but no child of her own. Perhaps if she had, she might not have had the time for all her "book children," nor as much love for the many thousands who wrote to her, who considered her their great confidante and friend.

A Wish for Connection

Although many great children's books have been written over many hundreds of years, the field of children's literature has been woefully overlooked by scholars until recently, according to Professor Marek Oziewicz, the Sidney and Marguerite Henry Professor of Children's and Young Adult Literature at the University of Minneapolis Minnesota.

Professor Oziewicz admires *King of the Wind,* which he calls a particularly remarkable book for its multicultural emphasis written at a time when such works were rare, almost unheard of in children's literature. "It's fiction slash nonfiction and genealogy too," Professor Oziewicz observed. "The horse has personality, subjectivity, and grit, much like his human counterpart, Agba." Marguerite also created heroes who overcame impossible odds, he noted. She knew how to use "one of the most successful formulas in literature—orphans overcoming unimaginable odds and rising to greatness by realizing their full potential."

Professor Dawn Heinecken, Professor and Chairperson of Women's, Gender and Sexuality Studies at the University of Louisville, grew up riding horses and reading Marguerite's books and is also a scholar of her work. She wrote a 2017 study on Marguerite's writing—perhaps the first of its kind. Entitled "Contact Zones: Humans, Horses and the Stories of Marguerite Henry," Heinecken found that Marguerite's books *articulate the significant otherness of horses and humans, deconstructing human fantasies about nonhuman animals while suggesting their shared kinship and communication.* " Marguerite's novels *"encourage kindness towards animals and acknowledge (and value) their existence separate and distinct from humans but leave no specific rules as to how humans and animals should interact,"* Heinecken wrote.

When she re-read Marguerite's books as an adult, Heinecken was impressed anew by their ethical messages, said Heinecken. *"There is just something deeper in her books,"* adding that she thought because Marguerite was a woman writing a certain sort of book in a certain time period that her books have been overlooked by critics, even today. But Marguerite's message is more important, more urgent than ever, Heinecken emphasized. *"Recognizing the autonomy of animals is an important part of her message—that's even more critical now."*

While Marguerite may have written her books many decades ago, when the world was (or at least seemed to be) a much less fractured, less terrifying place, her stories with their ethical messages have endured because they spark a timeless wish for connection—and love— not only with her characters and animals (mostly horses), but also with the author herself. Marguerite was a bestselling author, a minor celebrity, and a tireless researcher of history and horses, but she transcended all such titles to be something else perhaps even more powerful: a reader's best friend.

letters

The biographer, age fifteen

WHAT
MARGUERITE HENRY
MEANT TO ME

EPILOGUE

"The things which a child loves remain in the domain of the heart until old age."

—

Kahlil Gibran, *Mirrors of the Soul*

AS a horse-obsessed young girl, I read over a dozen Marguerite Henry books (*Born to Trot* was my particular favorite) and collected a stable full of Breyer model horses, including Misty and Justin Morgan. Like Marguerite, I pined for a horse of my own. But unlike Marguerite, after seven years of once-a-week riding lessons, I was able to buy one. I was sixteen years old when I bought a four-year-old, chestnut, "green-broke" Quarter Horse mare named Lady for four hundred dollars with my own money earned one summer working at a crepe stand.

More horses (and one pony) followed—all of whom were quite cheap and thus little or badly trained—but just a few years later, I had to sell them all when my father lost his job. It would be many (many) years before I would again have a horse of my own—not once but twice.

Those are horse stories for another time.

During one of my horse-less years I took an interest in the horse-crazy daughters of friends, especially my friends Liz and Greg's then-eight-year-old daughter Samantha ("Sam"). One day, while visiting their house, I found Sam reading *Misty of Chincoteague.* How had Sam ended up reading a book from my own childhood, which I thought of as so long ago? I had no idea that *Misty* still appealed to young horse lovers some eighty years after the book debuted.

The fact that Marguerite Henry's words were resonant so many decades after she wrote them is nothing short of remarkable. And yet, while her books clearly had endured, I wondered, whatever had happened to Marguerite Henry herself? I wanted to know. I did a bit of basic research (aka Googling) but couldn't find very much. There were a few articles, and a bare-bones Wikipedia profile. How could a writer as prolific and acclaimed as Marguerite Henry have failed to attract a biographer?

Just a month before the COVID-19 pandemic hit in March 2020, I began researching the writer's life in earnest, beginning with a trip to the Elmer L. Andersen Library at the University of

Minnesota in Minneapolis, where the Marguerite Henry papers are kept. From there I traveled directly to Wayne, Illinois, where I made the acquaintance of Art Richardson, an old neighbor and friend of Marguerite's who still lives down the road from what was once Marguerite's house. Art took me to the Henry house and around the yard Marguerite had dubbed Mole Meadow (the current owners weren't home), and we went other places in Wayne as well, including the Wayne Hunt Club where Marguerite and Sid were members and where Art had once been Master of the Hounds.

In the months and years that followed—some of them in full-blown pandemic shutdown—I found more and more people who knew Marguerite personally or had loved her books as I had. They were horse people and writers and librarians and descendants of characters who had appeared in Marguerite's books. Some were distant relations of Marguerite's—still living in Wisconsin, the state of her birth—and some were writers and artists who became friends with Marguerite in the later stages of her life. They all generously shared memories and stories, some of which made it into this book, and others, for one reason or another, sadly did not. But every memory they shared helped me gain a better understanding of Marguerite as a person and a friend, a wife and horse lover, and of course a writer who left an indelible mark on their lives—as she did on mine.

I wonder if every biographer feels a touch bereft, as I did, when it was finally time to let go of their subject's life, leaving certain questions unanswered, certain mysteries unsolved. But there were always the words—the books—that Marguerite left behind. I read and re-read her books and found magic there every time—there is so much feeling, so much beauty in her prose. And so, it is only fitting that I end this book with her words and not my own.

"

On this clear spring morning
the wind is livelier than usual,
swirling the grasses into sea-green whirlpools,
now pale, now dark. Quail scuttle
and bob along, making whispers in the grass.
And wild turkeys fly above the fields,
squawking their praise to the morning.

—

FROM

BLACK GOLD

"

ACKNOWLEDGMENTS

There are so many people to whom I am equal parts indebted and grateful and without whom this book would never have been brought to life.

First, a million thanks to the people who brought me closest to Marguerite: Catherine McClure, the "keeper of the flame"; Eugenia Snyder and Art Richardson, who became friends as well as frequent telephone pals. Also: Mary Jon Quayle Edwards, John Mooney, Benny White, Lee Smith, Ed Richardson, Susan Foster, Peter Stone, Nancy Winter, Fred Voght, Ann Kekonen,

Bonnie Shields, Devon Settle, and Janet Secrest, all of whom shared their own Marguerite stories.

Thanks to Marek Oziewicz, Professor and Sidney and Marguerite Henry Chair of Children's Literature, University of Minnesota Minneapolis; Lisa Von Drasek, Curator Children's Research Collections, University of Minnesota Minneapolis; David Haynes, Milwaukee journalist; John Gurda, Milwaukee historian; Steven Scaffer, Milwaukee County Historical Society; Dawn Heinecken, Professor and Chairperson of Women's Gender & Sexuality Studies, University of Louisville; Stephanie Macejko, Breyer Animal Creations; The Misty of Chincoteague Foundation; The Wayne Historical Society; Michael Musson, Wayne Township; Graham Geer, The Newbery Library; Cindy Faith, Executive Director of the Museum of Chincoteague Island; Lydia Nixon, Lilly Library of the University of Indiana; Sherri Price Bruen, historian; Jon Anderson, President and Publisher of the Simon & Schuster Children's Publishing Division; and the Bobbs-Merrill and Rand McNally archives.

Huge thanks to Trafalgar Square Books—Martha Cook and Rebecca Didier, aka "Team Marguerite," who loved the idea of this book immediately, if not sooner—and to Alice Martell, book agent extraordinaire. Thanks so very much to Katarzyna Misiukanis–Celińska for her brilliant book design. And thank you, Samantha Weber, for inspiring the search that eventually led to this book.

Thanks to all the horses in my life, past and present, but especially to the aptly named "Tenderly."

And last, but far from least, thank you to my husband Roger Drill who makes my life a daily joy.

BIBLIOGRAPHY

- American Morgan Horse Association. "The Life and Times of Figure." Last modified December 25, 2020. https://www.morganhorse.com/about/museum/ the-life-and-times-of-figure/
- Arnor, Mark. "Rancho Santa Fe Author Remains Novel Writer for Children." *San Diego Tribune*, January 16, 1992.
- *Austin American-Statesman* (TX). "Young Book World," review of *San Domingo: The Medicine Hat Stallion,* by Marguerite Henry and Robert Lougheed. December 10, 1972.
- Beall, Abby. "The Art of Wesley Dennis." Last modified December 24, 2010. http:// wesleydennis.com
- Bren, Paulina. *The Barbizon: The Hotel That Set Women Free.* New York: Simon & Schuster, 2022.
- Broady, Joe. "Annie's Their Friend: Wild Horses Have a 'Drag'." *Daily Oklahoman*, September 21, 1967.
- Burroughs, John. *Summit of the Years.* Boston: Houghton Mifflin, 1913.
- Bustin, John. "Show World." *Austin American-Statesman* (TX), June 8, 1967.
- *Californian* (Salinas, CA). "Fred Tejan Rites Held" (obituary). December 9, 1955.
- *Cardunal Free Press* (IL). "Brighty To Appear In Dundee Saturday." January 17, 1968.
- *Carpinteria Herald* (CA). "'Author-go-round' successful event." May 23, 1974.
- Chapman, Jesse. "Off Stage With Jesse Chapman: 'Misty' of Chincoteague." *World-News* (Roanoke, VA), May 13, 1961.
- Coolidge, Elizabeth S. "Books for the Young: Lovable critters," review of *San Domingo: The Medicine Hat Stallion*, by Marguerite Henry and Robert Lougheed. *Boston Globe*, February 3, 1973.
- Cruise, David, and Alison Griffiths. *Wild Horse Annie and the Last of the Mustangs.* New York: Scribner, 2010.

- *Daily Ardmoreite* (OK). "Osage Indian Woman Passes." April 25, 1938.

- *Daily Herald* (IL). "Police Catch 2 Going 95, 105 mph on Route 120." July 27, 1957.

- *Daily Herald* (CO). "Sidney Drexler" (obituary). September 17, 2016.

- *Daily News* (NY). "John Wesley Dennis" (obituary). September 5, 1966.

- *Daily Mail* (MD). "Count Shows 55 Ponies Dead On Chincoteague." March 12, 1962.

- *Daily Oklahoman.* "True-to-Life Story Told: 'Wild Horse Annie' Feted."
  September 22, 1967.

- *Daily Times* (MD). "75 Bulldozers Dig At Resort." March 10, 1962.

- *Daily Times* (MD). "Misty" movie advertisement. June 15, 1961.

- *Daily Times* (MD). "Misty Foals For Third Time." March 12, 1962.

- *Daily Times* (MD). "Misty Is Safe, 75 Ponies On Island Spotted." March 9, 1962.

- *Daily Times* (MD). "Misty's Third Colt Is Due." March 10, 1962.

- *Daily Times* (MD). "Ponies May Have Been Wiped Out." March 8, 1962.

- Dennis, Wesley. *A Crow I Know.* New York: Viking Press, 1957.

- Dennis, Wesley. *Flip.* New York: Viking Press, 1941.

- Douglas, Archer Wall. "The Art and Nature of Graphology." *Atlantic Monthly*, March 1924.

- Dunham Woods Riding Club. "Our History." Last modified March 13, 2020. https://www.
  dunhamwoodsridingclub.com/Default.aspx?p=DynamicModule&pageid=57&ssid=
  100049&vnf=1

- Eastern Shore of Virginia Public Library System. "Mary 'Mollie' P. Rowley b. 3 Oct 1883
  Worcester Co, Maryland d. 30 Mar 1974 Worcester Co, Maryland: MilesFiles." Last
  modified 2024. https://espl-genealogy.org/getperson.php?personID=I128031&tree=1

- Fleshman, Charlotte. "Author Longed To Be a Horse." *Pantagraph* (IL), November 22, 1964.

- *Freeport Journal-Standard.* "News about People You Know." April 17, 1959.

- Gallagher, Hugh. "Film TV Pilot In New Mexico." *Albuquerque Journal*, August 14, 1977.

- Glueckstein, Fred. *Of Men, Women and Horses.* Bloomington, IN: Xlibris, 2006.

- Goodman, Bob. "Sights and Sounds: Early America; Lots of Sports." *Atlanta Constitution*,
  February 6, 1972.

- Goss, Judith. "Fashions and Fancy." *Chicago Tribune*, September 26, 1954.

- Graves, Sheri. "Marguerite Henry: She Writes UP to Children." *Press Democrat* (CA),
  November 20, 1966.

- Gurda, John (Milwaukee historian), in discussion with the author, 2023.

- *Hackensack Record* (NJ). "Horses and Dogs Most in Demand." March 18, 1949.

- Hawksbee, Bruce. "Change of pace for Hawthorne." *Evening Telegraph* (Derby,
  UK), May 21, 1990.

- Heinecken, Dawn. "Contact Zones: Humans, Horses, and the Stories of Marguerite Henry."
  Children's Literature Association Quarterly 42, no. 1 (2017): 21-42.

- Henry, Marguerite. "About a Shaggy Little Fellow Who Wears and Bears a Cross." *Chicago
  Tribune,* November 15, 1953.

- Henry, Marguerite. "The Baker's Dozen." (unpublished personal document, April 26, 1968).
  Typed manuscript.

- Henry, Marguerite. *Dear Readers and Riders.* Chicago: Rand McNally, 1969.

- Henry, Marguerite. "The Four-Footed Professor" (personal essay). 1964.

- Henry, Marguerite. "Horse Sense Is Stable Thinking." *Wayne-DuPage Hunt Newsletter*, 1928–1980.

- Henry, Marguerite. "Newbery Medal Acceptance," award acceptance speech, American Library Association Midwest Regional Conference in Grand Rapids, MI, November 9–12, 1949.

- Henry, Marguerite. "Those Who Carry Umbrellas." *Book Bulletin*. Chicago Public Library, 1956.

- Henry, Marguerite. "Turning Points in the Lives of Famous Men." Pts 1–3, *Saturday Evening Post*, 1935–1939.

- Henry, Marguerite. "Twenty Questions and Answers" (unpublished personal document, undated). Typed manuscript.

- Henry, Marguerite. "A Weft of Truth and a Warp of Fiction." *Elementary English 51* (October 1974): 920–25.

- Henry, Marguerite, and Bonnie Shields. *Brown Sunshine of Sawdust Valley*. New York: Simon & Schuster, 1996.

- Henry, Marguerite, and Diana Thorne. *The Little Fellow*. New York: Holt Rhinehart & Winston, 1945.

- Henry, Marguerite, and Gladys Rourke Blackwood. *Auno and Tauno: A Story of Finland*. Chicago: Albert Whitman, 1940.

- Henry, Marguerite, and Gladys Rourke Blackwood. *Dilly Dally Sally*. Akron, OH: Saalfield Publishing Company, 1940.

- Henry, Marguerite, and Gladys Rourke Blackwood. *Geraldine Belinda*. New York: Platt & Munk, 1942.

- Henry, Marguerite, and Karen Haus Grandpré. *Misty's Twilight*. New York: Macmillan, 1992.

- Henry, Marguerite, and Lawrence T. Dresser. *Robert Fulton, Boy Craftsman*. Indianapolis: Bobbs-Merrill, 1945.

- Henry, Marguerite, and Lynd Ward. *Gaudenzia, Pride of the Palio*. Chicago: Rand McNally, 1960.

- Henry, Marguerite, and Robert Lougheed. *Mustang: Wild Spirit of the West*. Chicago: Rand McNally, 1966.

- Henry, Marguerite, and Robert Lougheed. *San Domingo: The Medicine Hat Stallion*. Chicago: Rand McNally, 1972.

- Henry, Marguerite, and Wesley Dennis. *Album of Horses*. Chicago: Rand McNally, 1951.

- Henry, Marguerite, and Wesley Dennis. *Benjamin West and His Cat Grimalkin*. Indianapolis: Bobbs-Merrill, 1947.

- Henry, Marguerite, and Wesley Dennis. *Black Gold*. Chicago: Rand McNally, 1957.

- Henry, Marguerite, and Wesley Dennis. *Born to Trot*. Chicago: Rand McNally, 1950.

- Henry, Marguerite, and Wesley Dennis. *Brighty of the Grand Canyon*. Chicago: Rand McNally, 1953.

- Henry, Marguerite, and Wesley Dennis. *Cinnabar: The One O'Clock Fox*. Chicago: Rand McNally, 1956.

- Henry, Marguerite, and Wesley Dennis. *Five O'Clock Charlie*. Chicago: Rand McNally, 1962.

- Henry, Marguerite, and Wesley Dennis. *Justin Morgan Had a Horse*. New York: Wilcox & Follett, 1945.

- Henry, Marguerite, and Wesley Dennis. *King of the Wind*. Chicago: Rand McNally, 1948.

- Henry, Marguerite, and Wesley Dennis. *Misty of Chincoteague*. Chicago: Rand McNally, 1947.

- Henry, Marguerite, and Wesley Dennis. *A Pictorial Life Story of Misty*. Chicago: Rand McNally, 1976.

- Henry, Marguerite, and Wesley Dennis. *Sea Star, Orphan of Chincoteague.* Chicago: Rand McNally, 1949.

- Henry, Marguerite, and Wesley Dennis. *Stormy: Misty's Foal.* Chicago: Rand McNally, 1963.

- Henry, Marguerite, and Wesley Dennis. *White Stallion of Lipizza.* Chicago: Rand McNally, 1964.

- Henry, Marguerite, with Wesley Dennis, Robert Lougheed, Lynd Ward, and Rich Rudish. *The Illustrated Marguerite Henry.* Chicago: Checkerboard Press and Rand McNally, 1980.

- *Hollywood Sun-Tattler* (FL). "Foxy, Fast Antics of Cinnabar Authored During Hollywood Visit." November 15, 1956.

- *Hollywood Sun-Tattler* (FL). "Swedish Saying Paces Talk." February 18, 1957.

- Illinois Prairie Path Not-for-Profit Corporation. "Illinois Prairie Path – Founded in 1963." Last modified January 28, 2024. https://ipp.org

- *Independent* (Long Beach, CA). "Cowboy Friend of Will Rogers Stricken, Dies" (obituary). December 9, 1955.

- *Independent Republican.* (NY). "Death of Old Hambletonian" (obituary). Undated.

- *Index-Journal* (SC). "Famous Horse To Be Stuffed." October 18, 1972.

- *Indianapolis Star.* L.S. Ayres & Co advertisement including copy for *Stormy: Misty's Foal,* by Marguerite Henry and Wesley Dennis. November 18, 1963.

- Jaffe, Matt. "The Tale of a Donkey." *Arizona Highways,* January 2022.

- Jones, Dorothy. "Tale Of Royal Horse Pulling Cart Wins Newbery Prize," review of *King of the Wind,* by Marguerite Henry and Wesley Dennis. *Jackson Sun* (TN), September 4, 1949.

- Jones, George O., Norman S. McVean, and others, comp. *The History of Lincoln, Oneida and Vilas Counties.* Minneapolis: H.C. Cooper Jr., 1924.

- Jupp, Gertrude. "My little sister Marguerite Henry." *Horn Book Magazine,* January–February 1950.

- Kimelman, Donald. "Museum displays stuffed heroine: Misty comes home to Chincoteague." *Baltimore Sun,* August 4, 1975.

- Kindy, Dave. "DNA evidence may link Chincoteague pony origins to Spanish shipwreck." *Washington Post,* August 6, 2022.

- Kuhn, Luvada. "Book reviews: Two books for young readers," review of *San Domingo: The Medicine Hat Stallion,* by Marguerite Henry and Robert Lougheed. *Chillicothe Gazette* (OH), June 30, 1973.

- *Lansing State Journal* (MI). Review of *King of the Wind,* by Marguerite Henry and Wesley Dennis. December 19, 1948.

- Layton, Bob. "Misty Premiere Produces Pony for Caroline Kennedy." *Daily Times* (MD), June 15, 1961.

- Leader, Julie. "Author Says: Animals Kinder Than Humans." *Dayton Daily News* (OH), October 19, 1964.

- *Ledger-Star* (VA). "Chincoteague Man Killed." April 5, 1957.

- Leigh, Michael. Review of *Justin Morgan Had a Horse,* by Marguerite Henry. *Pensacola News-Journal,* October 17, 1954.

- Leskovitz, Frank J. "Diana Thorne Artist." Last modified May 3, 2011. http://dianathorne.com

- Libby, Margaret Sherwood. "For Boys & Girls: Pretty good in a cinch," review of *White Stallion of Lipizza,* by Marguerite Henry and Wesley Dennis. *San Francisco Examiner,* August 1, 1965.

- Lindeman, Edith. "'Family Entertainment' Trial Is Cast in a Virginia Setting." *Richmond Times-Dispatch* (VA), May 14, 1961.

- Linsley, Faith B., and Stella Brooks. "Book Reviews," review of *Black Gold*, by Marguerite Henry and Wesley Dennis. *Barre Daily Times* (VT), December 11, 1957.

- Loring, Kay. "Author Henry, Like Her Readers, Charmed by Her Animals," Front Views and Profiles. *Chicago Tribune*, April 11, 1962.

- Martin, Allie Beth. "Research Job." *Tulsa World*, November 24, 1957.

- Martin, Fran. "Roundup of Children's Books," review of *Black Gold*, by Marguerite Henry and Wesley Dennis. *Virginian-Pilot*, November 17, 1957.

- McKee, Thomas Heron. "Brighty, Free Citizen: How the Sagacious Hermit Donkey of the Grand Canyon Maintained His Liberty for Thirty Years." *Sunset Magazine*, August 1922.

- Miller, Lucy Key. "Front Views & Profiles: Carrots for Candles." *Chicago Tribune*, July 17, 1952.

- Miller, Lucy Key. "Front Views & Profiles: Birthday of a Book." *Chicago Tribune*, October 18, 1950.

- *Minneapolis Star.* "Writer of Children's Books Visits City." December 3, 1966.

- Mooar, Brian. "'Misty' Author Marguerite Henry Dies at 95." *Washington Post*, November 27, 1997.

- Morey, Helen. "Craze for Horses Lasts in Books." *Standard Star* (New Rochelle, NY), June 9, 1950.

- Naus, Leone M. "Shopping with Leone," review of *Born to Trot*, by Marguerite Henry and Wesley Dennis. *Sheboygan Press* (WI), November 15, 1950.

- *New York Herald Tribune Weekly Book Review.* Review of *Little Fellow*, by Marguerite Henry and Wesley Dennis. May 20, 1945.

- Oleksy, Walt. "Vienna Still the City of Your Dreams." *Chicago Tribune*, April 5, 1959.

- *Omaha World Herald.* Review of *Born to Trot*, by Marguerite Henry and Wesley Dennis. December 10, 1950.

- Orbach, Ruth. "The Children's Bookshelf," review of *White Stallion of Lipizza*, by Marguerite Henry and Wesley Dennis. *Herald-News* (NJ), December 24, 1964.

- *Pantagraph* (IL). "Frances Baker Initiates New Era at Fairview." November 9, 1947.

- *Pantagraph* (IL). "Lipizzan Stallions Dance Through Marguerite Henry's Latest Book," review of *White Stallion of Lipizza*, by Marguerite Henry and Wesley Dennis. November 22, 1964.

- Perry, Helen J. "Author Waits Expectantly for Famed 'Misty's' First Foal." *News Journal* (Wilmington, DE), March 17, 1960.

- Phillips, Dolores. "Circling the Countryside: A Thrill for the Children." *Evening Star* (DC), June 18, 1961.

- Rand McNally. "Dear Readers and Riders," newsletter issues 1–9. 1965-1969.

- Regan, Mary Beth. "Era draws to close at home of 'Misty'." *Daily Press* (VA), July 26, 1989.

- *Richmond News Leader* (VA). "Trial Date Set for Richardson in Slaying Case." November 18, 1938.

- *Richmond Times-Dispatch* (VA). "John Wesley Dennis, 63, Dies; Illustrator of Horse Books." September 5, 1966.

- Ross, Jean V. "Children's Author Bases Her Books on Life." *Courier-Post* (NJ), November 21, 1964.

- Ryon, Ruth. "Horse is a horse unless it's a Morgan—a Morgan?!" *Daily News-Post* (CA), February 11, 1972.

- *Sacramento Bee.* "Even After Death Misty Will Stand In Her Stall." October 18, 1972.

- *Santa Ynez Valley News.* "At Santa Ynez: Children of Valley Schools To Attend 'Author-Go-Round'." April 11, 1974.

- *San Francisco Examiner.* "Velma 'Wild Horse Annie' Johnston" (obituary). June 28, 1977.

- Saunders, Mark. "After 50 years, Misty of Chincoteague is still the centerpiece of island's dogged pony show." *Daily Times* (MD), July 21, 1996.

- Schaden, Herman. "Chincoteague Casualty: Oystermen Out of Business." *Evening Star* (DC), March 13, 1962.

- Schaeffer, Steve (historian, Milwaukee Historical Society), in discussion with the author, 2023

- Selvin, Molly. "'Misty' Rides Again, Charming Children," *Los Angeles Times*, July 23, 1992.

- Semrad, Alberita R. "Favorite Authors Write New Stories of Horses," review of *Black Gold*, by Marguerite Henry and Wesley Dennis. *Chicago Tribune,* November 17, 1957.

- *Skiatook News* (OK). "Seeking 'Info' about Skiatook and Black Gold." March 14, 1957.

- *Something about the Author*, ed. Joyce Nakamura, vol. 7. Detroit: Gale, 1989.

- *South Wales Evening Post* (Swansea, UK). "King of the Wind" movie advertisement. May 25, 1990.

- Stallsmith, Pamela. "Saluting a legend: Family, others will honor 'Misty' author Henry." *Richmond Times-Dispatch* (VA), December 7, 1997.

- Sutherland, Zena, ed. "Children's Books," review of *San Domingo: The Medicine Hat Stallion*, by Marguerite Henry and Robert Lougheed. *Chicago Tribune*, November 5, 1972.

- Tamisiea, Jack. "Beloved Chincoteague ponies' mythical origins may be real." *National Geographic*, July 27, 2022.

- Taylor, Craig E. "'I've Never Met A Stranger': So Says Fred Tejan, The Oklahoma Cowboy Who's Playing Polo In The Green Spring Valley." *Baltimore Sun*, August 15, 1948.

- Thomas, Jane. "Horse Story Kept Real," review of *Stormy, Misty's Foal,* by Marguerite Henry and Wesley Dennis. *Star Tribune* (MN), February 9, 1964.

- *The Tri-States Union.* (NY). "The Decease of Harmon Showers" (obituary). March 17, 1898.

- Tucker, Leigh. "Ben White Horse Stars in Book." *Orlando Evening Star,* April 10, 1950.

- UiBreaslain, Neil. *The Way of an Irish Horseman.* Bloomington, IN: AuthorHouse, 2006.

- *Wichita Falls Times* (TX). "In Books for Boys: Repeat Performance by Well-Loved Authors," review of *Cinnabar, The One O'Clock Fox,* by Marguerite Henry and Wesley Dennis. December 16, 1956.

- Williams, Emma Inman, ed. "Marguerite Henry Takes Her Readers To Land Of Wild Mustangs In Fine Tale," review of *Mustang: Wild Spirit of the West,* by Marguerite Henry and Robert Lougheed. *Jackson Sun* (TN), November 13, 1966.

- Williams, Leonore P. "Display Christmas Books for Children," review of *Brighty of the Grand Canyon,* by Marguerite Henry and Wesley Dennis. *Ludington Daily News* (MI), December 10, 1953.

- Yager, Elisabeth. "Author of Many Successful Books for Children Wrote First One Here." *Freeport Journal-Standard*, November 9, 1948.

INDEX

Numbers for photo plates, in *italics*,
correspond to numbered images
in the photo insert pages.